To

Dear Nithin & Nishaan,

With love
ARJUNA

# The Bhagavad Gita

*Retold by*
**M. D. Gupta**

*Edited by*
**S. P. Singh**

*Illustrated by*
**N. K. Vikram**

*Published by:*

**DREAMLAND PUBLICATIONS**

J-128, Kirti Nagar, New Delhi -110 015  (India)
Phone : 011-2510 6050,  Fax : 011-2543 8283
E-mail :  dreamland@vsnl.com
www.dreamlandpublications.com

Published in 2007 by
**DREAMLAND PUBLICATIONS**
J-128, Kirti Nagar, New Delhi - 110 015 (India)
Tel : 011-2510 6050, Fax : 011-2543 8283
E-mail : dreamland@vsnl.com, www.dreamlandpublications.com

ISBN 81-7301-236-9

Printed by

**EIH** LIMITED

A member of The Oberoi Group
UNIT PRINTING PRESS

# PREFACE

There is no gain-saying that the Bhagavad Gita contains the divine words, directly emanating from the lips of Lord Shri Krishna. Its glory is infinite. The great scholars all over the world, have declared the Gita as an epitome of all the holy Scriptures. It contains the essence of all the four Vedas. It embodies the supreme spiritual truth as well as many unfathomed mysteries.

The divine Sage Veda Vyasa says : "The Gita alone should be sung, heard, recited, studied, taught, pondered and assimilated properly and well" (Mahabharata Bhisma Parva 43.1).

Some critics consider the Gita far superior to the holy Ganga River and the Gayatri Mantra. This book is an unfathomable ocean of wisdom. It is the main fountain-head of inspiration to all the people who become dumb-founded and inactive like Arjuna in the battle of the Mahabharata. The Gita leads all its devoted readers towards the self-realization or the supreme deliverance from the worldly bondage by following the unique paths of 'Knowledge', 'Worship' and 'Action'. The devoted readers of the Gita attain perfect bliss, purity of mind and ultimate union or 'Symbiosis' with God.

The Dreamland Publishers are presenting the Bhagavad Gita in a very simple and elegant style for the benefit of the young readers. The beauty of the book has been enhanced by the captivating pictures, painted by their famous artist, Mr. N. K. Vikram who has clarified the theme of the Gita effectively.

It is hoped that this book will do the greatest good to the greatest number of people in the world.

# CONTENTS

# 1. GITA—THE DIVINE MOTHER

The Gita has been called the Divine Mother who looks after the welfare and the upliftment of the whole mankind. Just like the Universal mother, she rises above all castes and creeds and embraces the human race in her loving arms. She is ever ready to shower her nectar on all the children of the whole world.

The Gita is a unique scripture of mankind. He who reads it, is uplifted to a higher realm of happiness.

Mahatma Gandhi, the Father of the Indian Nation, considered the Gita to be his eternal mother. He says in a famous and well-known passage:

"The Gita is my mother. I lost my earthly mother who gave me birth long ago. But this eternal mother has completely filled her place by my side. She has never failed me. Whenever I am in difficulty or distress, I seek refuge in her bosom." In fact, the people of the whole world can seek solace and succour by a study of the Gita. The Gita does not differentiate people on the basis of caste, colour, creed, religion or sex. So, the Christians, the Muslims, the Buddhists, the Zoroastrians and the Hindus can derive eternal bliss by pondering over the Verses of the Gita.

This divine mother teaches all her children living all over the world how to live in love, peace and prosperity. Life is one and the same everywhere.

There are eighteen chapters comprising of seven hundred Verses (Slokas) in the Bhagavad Gita. Even a single Verse, well-understood and acted upon in actual life, can solve each and every problem of man. The Gita has been translated in more than a hundred languages of the world.

If we approach the Divine Mother with folded hands in all humility like a child, she will feed us with her milk of wisdom which will put an end to all our sorrows, sufferings, troubles and tribulations. We shall be living in the heaven of joy.

The Bhagavad Gita is the divine gospel that India has given to all human-beings at all times and in all climes.

The Gita is a commentary on the Upanishadas. There are about 108 Upanishadas which deal with the ultimate reality of life and death. But the language of the Upanishadas is so intricate and difficult that it cannot be understood easily. Moreover, the thoughts and ideas enshrined in them are so deep that they cannot be comprehended unless one sits at the feet of a learned man of realization.

Here appears, the Gita, in the role of Divine Mother. Its language is simple enough to be understood easily by a little practice and guidance.

Lord Krishna has milked the nectar of the Upanishadas for the benefit of the whole of mankind. The Gita is the nectar like milk which can be consumed and assimilated easily by one and all to strengthen themselves to face the battle of life with a smiling face at every step.

Why has the Gita been described as the milk of the Upanishadas ? There are many reasons for it. First of all, milk is a perfect and balanced food. It contains all the ingredients of a balanced diet. So, it is the same case with the Gita. It contains all that is necessary to make a man balanced and perfect. Secondly, milk is easily digestible and nourishing. When the body becomes the victim of diseases, the mind too loses its capacity to think clearly. Consequently, the intellect gets clouded, as it happened in the case of Arjuna on the battle-field of Kurukshetra.

He who drinks the easily digestible nectar-like milk of the Gita is nurtured and nourished in body, mind, intellect and spirit. All his problems and anxieties disappear. He discovers within his bosom the unfathomable and inexhaustible reservoir of strength. He becomes the master of his inner and the outer world, as was the case with Arjuna. Having drunk the milk of the Gita from the immortal hands of Lord Krishna, he sprang to his feet and became the very embodiment of Death to the mighty Kaurava forces. All the demoniac forces met their doom at the mighty hands of Arjuna.

What can be accomplished by one man in the person of Arjuna, can also be accomplished by all of us in the present day world. We, too, like Arjuna can conquer the whole host of the evil forces like Passion, Anger, Greed, Lust, Ignorance, Malice, Envy and the demon-like hundred sons of the blind Dhritrashtra residing within our own bosoms.

"Where is Lord Krishna ?" You will ask in a baffled tone. But a man of truth is never baffled. Lord Krishna is ever there within our own bosom. The Krishna consciousness is lying dormant within us. It means we are not aware of Krishna dwelling within our bosoms. But Krishna has never forgotten us and He shall never forget us come what may. He is the Main Actor behind all our activities.

It is He who sees through our eyes. It is He who hears through our ears. It is He who walks through the medium of our feet and legs. It is He who acts through our hands. It is He who perceives through the mind. It is He who takes vital decisions through the intellect. To sum up, the whole episode, it is none but Lord Krishna who pervades every atom of the Universe. He is there in the Wind, in the Oceans, on the Earth, in the Sky and in the Sun.

The neutrons and the protons are actually activated by the magic of His presence. He is the Presiding Deity of the whole Universe. The millions of other Universes which are yet to be discovered by man belong to Him alone. None can challenge Him. He alone is Omni-potent, Omni-scient and Omni-present. All glory and salutations unto Him. So, discover Krishna within to put an end to your tears and turmoil. But the crux of the problem is how to discover Him. The role of the Gita, the Mother Divine is indispensable in this context. She is impatiently waiting and inviting her earthly children to suckle in the nectarine milk from her breast to empower and purify the intellect.

When the mind and intellect are purified by drinking deep at the eternal Fountain of the Gita, Lord Krishna at once reveals Himself to hug man to His bosom. The immortal saint Kabir says, "The moment my mind became as pure as the holy and sacred waters of the Ganga, Krishna Himself started following me calling out 'O Kabir ! O Kabir ! where are you going ? I am left behind following you. Please pause and look back into my face."

In fact, he who knows Him merges in Him like the drop, falling into the ocean and becoming the ocean itself.

So, let us prostrate at the lotus-feet of the Divine Mother who shall bless us without fail with the vision of Lord Krishna Himself.

*Great is the glory of the Gita.* It has emanated from the lips of Lord Krishna Himself.

Even the Serpent-God Shesha Nag is not potent enough to sing the infinite and unlimited powers of the Gita. It is the essence of the four Vedas and the sweet kernel of the Mahabharata. It is known as the Fifth Veda. The students of the Gita must know that it occurs in the middle of the Mahabharata Epic. The human heart dwells in the middle of the body. If it stops throbbing, we are consigned to the flames of the pyre. The Gita, the central portion of the Mahabharata is the Heart of this great epic, nay, it is the Heart of Lord Krishna Himself. But for the Gita, the Mahabharata Epic would have been a dead book containing the ghastly tales of the dead warriors.

Undoubtedly, the Gita is the epitome of all the Scriptures that were there, and that would be in times to come. The immortal Sage Veda Vyasa himself says in the Bhishmaparva of the Mahabharta :

"The Gita alone should be sung, heard, recited, studied, taught, pondered over and assimilated properly. It is futile to collect other Scriptures because the Gita has emerged directly from the lotus-like lips of Lord Krishna Himself."

Lord Krishna Himself declares in the Varahapurana :

"I take my stand on the Gita. It is the Gita which is my supreme abode. I regulate and nourish the three worlds on the strength of the wisdom, enshrined in the Gita.

The Gita is there to lead us from darkness to light ; from falsehood to truth and from death to immortality.

Let us now prostrate at the lotus-feet of the Divine Mother to seek her blessings."

## 3. THE ESSENCE OF THE GITA

TAT-TWAM-ASI, the Great Incantation, is said to be the essence of the Gita. It means 'That, thou art.'

You are that God and nothing else. The Vedanta also proclaims this profound truth. So, the chapters 1 to 6 of the Gita explain Twam, the soul. The Chapters 7 to 12 explain Tat, God. The Chapters 13 to 18 explain the union and identity of the soul and God.

Thus, the Gita enables man to realise his true nature in three steps : (1) 1 am His ; (2) He is Mine and (3) He and I are one.

Now, our spiritual emancipation is imminent and near at hand, as we take up the study of each and every chapter of the Gita in brief in the upcoming pages of this book. Let us mind that brevity is the soul of wit.

The Mahabharta is called the fifth Veda because of the treasures of wisdom it contains. The Gita is an integral part of the Mahabharta. To understand the Gita, one must know, in brief, the background story of the main characters of the Mahabharta.

Before the Christian era, King Yudhishthira known as *Dharamraja* ruled over the powerful kingdom of Indraprastha. His four brothers—Bheema, Arjuna, Sahdeva and Nakula helped him in the matters of administration. They were the five sons of Pandu. So, they were called the Pandavas. They were very righteous and virtuous. The people of the kingdom lived in perfect peace and prosperity under their rule.

Once, King Yudhishthira performed the *Rajsuya Yajna* at the instance of his maternal cousin, Shri Krishna. A large number of smaller kings took part in it and all of them accepted the over-lordship of Emperor Yudhishthira. The Emperor's paternal cousin, Duryodhana also attended the Yajna. He could not tolerate the rise of Indraprashtha. He had been highly jealous of the Pandavas since his childhood.

When the evil-minded Duryodhana returned to his Capital Hastinapur, he began to nurse the idea of usurping the kingdom of Indraprashtha from the Pandavas. Shakuni, Duryodhana's maternal uncle was a cunning and crafty person. He was a past master at the dice-games. He asked Duryodhana to invite Yudhishthira to a game of dice so that he could be deprived of his powerful kingdom. Shakuni convinced Duryodhana, "I shall throw dice on your behalf in such a way that you shall be a winner every time."

"'But what would happen if Yudhishthira declined the invitation ?" was Duryodhana's next question. Shakuni explained, "Invitation to a game of dice is similar to a challenge for a battle and no self-respecting warrior can afford to decline it. Extend the invitation. Yudhishthira will accept it without fail. See, how I checkmate him and win his entire kingdom for you !" Duryodhana, the wicked, was fascinated by Shakuni's plan. He persuaded his blind father, King Dhritrashatra to extend the invitation to the Pandavas.

Having received the invitation for a game of dice, the five Pandavas reached Hastinapur. The game started. Shakuni-used enchanted dice and won each and every move. Soon, the Pandavas lost their powerful Kingdom. To win the kingdom back, Yudhisthira staked the beautiful Draupadi. But as ill luck would have it, she too was lost. All the five brothers lost themselves in the gamble. They became slaves. They could not wield their weapons. Draupadi, the Chaste, was insulted in the open Court by Duryodhana and his supporters. The Kaurava brothers did not realize that their deceitful gambling game and Draupadi's disgrace would bring their doom before long.

Shakuni decided to strike while the iron was still hot. So, he proposed to Yudhisthira, "Let us have another game. The losing side will have to pass twelve years in exile.

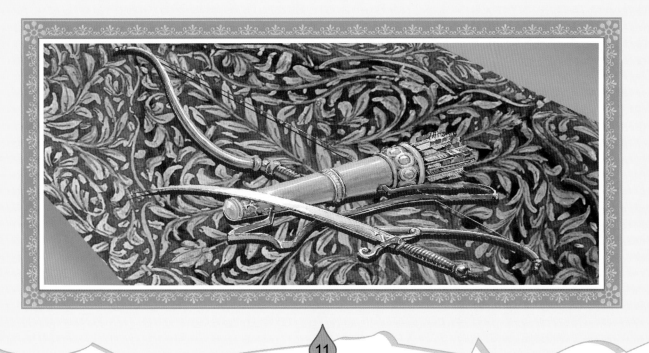

As for the thirteenth year, the losing side will have to remain untraceably underground. If traced, they will have to live in exile again for twelve years. After the expiry of this period, the losing side will regain their lost kingdom."

It is said that misfortunes never come alone. Yudhishthira lost this game as well. The Pandavas were jeered at. Dushasan, the wicked brother of Duryodhan ridiculed Draupadi saying, "Why should you, O King Drupad's daughter, suffer in exile along with these impotent Pandavas ? Leave them to their fate and marry anyone of the Kauravas who shall protect you."

Hearing Dushashan's taunt, Bheema roared, "O rogue, we have been defeated through deceit. 1, Kunti's son, take a vow to tear your chest in the battle-field and drink your blood. I will break the very thigh of your brother Duryodhana on which he had tried to seat Draupadi. My wrath shall not cool down until and unless I kill all your brothers. If I fail to accomplish all this, I shall forfeit my abode in heaven." When Kunti, the mother of the Pandavas, came to know that her sons were going into exile, she wept bitterly. The Pandavas could not stand the sight and left for their exile with heavy hearts.

Vidura, the learned Prime Minister of Hastinapur Kingdom, consoled Kunti, advising her to bow to God's will.

Dhritrashtra too had lost his peace of mind, as he knew well that his wicked sons would not be spared by the brave Pandavas. His guilty mind was constantly pricking his very conscience. He sent for Vidura and said to him, "Let me exactly know how Yudhishthira along with his brothers and Draupadi, proceeded to the forest."

Vidura replied, "My Lord, Yudhishthira, the eldest Pandava Prince is walking with his face covered with a piece of cloth and with his eyes almost shut. Bheema is walking abreast of him with his arms raised upwards. He is followed by Arjuna who while walking, is raising dust with his feet. Next is Sahdeva, Madri's son, who has besmeared his face with soil. Nakula, the youngest Pandava has besmeared with soil his entire body as well. Queen Draupadi weeping bitterly, is following the five brothers. She is hiding her face with her dishevelled hair. Last of all, walks saint Dhaumya, the Royal Priest of the Pandavas, holding blades of grass in his hands and chanting verses in praise of Lord Yama and Rudra."

Dhritrashtra was horrified to hear this description of the Pandavas going into exile. He asked wise Vidura to explain to him the deep meaning underlying these gestures on the part of the Pandavas.

Vidura retorted, "You are well aware of the fact, O King, that your sons have deprived the Pandavas of their Kingdom through deceit and deception. But Dharamraj Yudhisthira has not given up the path of virtue and righteousness. He still harbours in his heart a feeling of forgiveness for your sons. So, he has covered his face with a cloth to hide his wrath and anger. He is walking with almost shut eyes lest the fire of his red angry eyes should burn your sons to ashes. Bheema is walking with almost his arms raised high up to express that he would display his might, when the right moment comes for his valour."

Vidura continued, "Arjuna is following his two elder brothers raising dust with his feet to predict that he shall shower countless arrows at his enemies just as many as the particles of dust floating in the air. Sahdeva, the famous swordsman, has soiled his face to signify that he shall force his enemies lick dust on the battlefield. The most handsome, Nakula has besmeared his whole body with soil lest the on-looking ladies should fall in love with him.

Draupadi in her only saree, is walking with tears in her eyes and hair unkempt, to indicate that the wives of those, who are responsible for their disgrace in the open court, shall weep over their dead bodies just like her after thirteen years of exile. Dhaumya, the Royal Priest, is chanting verses in praise of Lord Yama, the God of Death, to indicate that Kripacharya shall be chanting similar verses when all the Kauravas meet their doom on the battle-field."

While Vidura was explaining all this to the King Dhritrashtra, people of Hastinapur were moaning aloud. They were exclaiming, "Alas ! our beloved Prince Yudhishthira along with his noble brothers and Queen Draupadi have been sent into exile. May God's curse befall the elders and nobles of his court."

A number of ominous happenings took place, as soon as the Pandavas advanced ahead on their way to the forest. *Lightning flashed without clouds in* the sky, the earth quaked and meteors fell on the right side of Hastinapur. *Jackals started howling.* Crows and vultures could be seen hovering in the sky, dropping bones and pieces of flesh on the minarets of forts, temples and high buildings.

Saint Narada who visited the Hastinapur Court, predicted the extermination of the Kuru dynasty, after a lapse of thirteen years.

The Pandavas remained in exile and in disguise for a period of twelve years. They stayed in the Capital of King Virata in the thirteenth year. Yudhishthira under the name of 'Kank' became King Virata's advisor. Bheema assumed the name of Vallabh and served as the Chief Royal Cook. The valiant Arjuna disguised himself as a eunuch named Brihnala. He became a music and dance teacher to Princess Uttara. Sahdeva looked after the cows and oxen of the King, while Nakula was in charge of the Royal Stable. Draupadi became the maid-servant of the Queen Sudeshna and assumed the name Sairandhari. What an irony of fate ! Man proposes but God disposes. Who can go against His will ? But then, what a patience on the part of the Pandavas ! They were on the path of true religion which protected them through their fiery ordeal.

As soon as the thirteenth year was over, the Pandavas disclosed their identity to King Virata. His joy knew no bounds. He felt himself to be as powerful as the Pandavas. So, he embraced Yudhishthira saying, "The entire Virata kingdom is at your disposal, O Great Pandava. Consider me to be one of your humble servants from today." As a token of his faithfulness to the Pandavas, King Virata gave his daughter Uttara to Arjuna's son Abhimanyu in marriage. This matrimonial alliance proved a boon to the Pandavas as well as to King Virata.

The Pandavas, then, settled at a place, named Upplavya which was an integral part of Virata's kingdom. Messengers were sent to all the friendly rulers who were asked to reach Upplavya with their respective armies. Plans were discussed to regain the lost kingdom of the Pandavas. The Royal Priest of King Drupada was sent to Hastinapur to negotiate a settlement with the Kaurvas. Having reached the Hastinapur Court, the Royal Priest pleaded to King Dhritrashtra, "Your Honour, you are well aware of the rules and regulations in vogue since time immemorial. The Pandavas have fulfilled all the conditions, imposed upon them by the game of dice. Now, they deserve their kingdom back. In spite of all their sufferings, they still believe in peace and friendship. They have sent me to request you to restore their kingdom to them."

The Grand-Sire Bhishma supported what the messenger had said. But Karna opposed it tooth and nail. He favoured Duryodhana who was bent upon retaining the kingdom of the Pandavas for himself. Tempers ran high and heated debates took place in the court. Confusion and commotion prevailed. King Dhrithrashtra decided to send his faithful charioteer, Sanjay, as a messenger to the Pandavas. Having reached Yudhishthira's Court at Upplavya, Sanjay duly greeted everybody present there and observed, "O Dharmaraja, my master King Dhritrashtra is eager to know about your welfare.

He hates war and desires peace. But my master's sons are all idiots. They do not pay any heed to the sane advice of their father and the great grandfather Bhishma. May I request you not to resort to war, as it is going to be a fratricidal one. Kindly stick to the path of forgiveness and righteousness even if Duryodhana refuses to give back your kingdom to you."

Yudhishthira replied, "Sanjay ! verily the path of virtue is the best for all to follow. Krishna, being the very embodiment of Religion, is a well-wisher of both the sides. I promise to abide by what he advises."

Having heard Yudhishthira, Shri Krishna observed, "Though I love the Pandavas, yet I have no intention of harming the Kaurvas. I want a peaceful settlement so that neither side suffers. I deem it proper to pay a personal visit to Hastinapur with my mission of peace. I will assure Dhritrashtra on behalf of the Pandavas that they shall serve him with devotion and dedication."

The moment Sanjay got ready to leave for Hastinapur, Yudhishthira requested him, "Sanjay, convey my profound regards to the Grand-Sire Bhishma and to our great revered Guru Drona. Tell dear Duryodhana, that we have forgotten all the sufferings and the disgrace of Draupadi in the open court, Kindly request him to be wise and just enough to return our kingdom."

"If he does not wish to restore the whole of our kingdom to us, we shall be satisfied if he grants us only five villages for our livelihood."

What a gesture of goodwill and contentment on the part of the Pandavas !

In due course of time, *Lord Krishna, the missionary of peace, reached the Hastinapur Court. No sooner did he step into the court than all present there stood up in His honour.* Having paid everyone his due regards, Krishna seated Himself and addressed King Dhritrashtra, "Do not choose, O King, the path that leads to utter destruction. As a father, it is your duty to guide your sons to the path of truth and justice. Though, by nature, the Pandvas are peace-loving yet by no means and standards they are cowards. They honour you just like a father. They wish to live under your loving care. Kindly accept them as your own sons so that there remains no scope for any ill-will and injustice."

The blind King Dhritrashtra retorted, "O Krishna, I too desire as you do. But I feel helpless as my sons are too obstinate to act upon my advice. Will you kindly advise Duryodhana to come to the right path ?"

Lord Krishna, now, turned to Duryodhana and said to him, "You are the descendant of a great dynasty of the Noble Kings. Does it behove you to behave in such a mean manner ? People fear that your misdeeds shall spell the doom of the powerful kingdom of the Kurus. So, justice demands that you must hand over the kingdom of the Pandavas to them without any further delay."

The learned Bhishma and the great Guru Dronacharya advised Duryodhana to act upon what Krishna had told him. But the wicked Prince denounced even Lord Krishna saying, "You always support the Pandavas without any rhyme or reason. It is your very nature to put all the blame on me. But I am absolutely blameless. The Pandavas gambled away their kingdom and you blame me for that loss. I am not to be cowed down by any threats of war. I am ever ready to wage a war against the Pandavas. Tell them I will not give them, any territory, even equal to the tip of a needle, at any cost."

Lord Krishna got enraged and retorted, "Listen, Duryodhan, You conspired with your maternal uncle Shakuni to deprive the Pandavas of their kingdom by using enchanted dice. Were you not intsrumental in disgracing Draupadi ? Did you not plan to burn the Pandavas alive while fast asleep ? Did you not poison Bheema in a treacherous way ? Don't you feel ashamed of yourself ?"

All those who were present in the Court supported Lord Krishna. It enraged Duryodhana who left the Court along with some of his supporters. All of them planned to imprison Krishna as soon as he happened to come out of the court. But the Omni-scient, Omni-potent and Omni-present Krishna could at once read their minds. The Lord assumed his *colossal/cosmic form* which was accompanied by unprecedented thunder. Seeing this dreadful form, a wave of fear ran among the courtiers. The *radiance of a thousand Suns bursting forth all, at once, blinded them. They* shut their eyes and bowed their heads in reverence. The evil designs of Duryodhana were of no avail. Krishna mounted His chariot and proceeded to Upplavya.

The Pandavas were eagerly waiting for Lord Krishna who told them that His mission of peace had miserably failed. Duryodhana would not give them anything without a bloody war.

Yudhisthira addressed his brothers thus, "As all the doors of peace, have been shut upon us, prepare the army and get ready to fight."

Dhrishtadyumn, the Panchal Prince (Draupadi's brother) was chosen the Commander of the Pandava's army.

On the other hand, Duryodhana appointed Bhishma, *the invincible, the Commander-in-Chief of the* Kaurva forces, as no one could kill him unless he himself desired to die.

Both the armies marched to the battle-field of Kurukshetra to meet their fate. Arjuna surrendered himself to Lord Krishna who chose to drive his chariot.

He who surrenders himself unto the Lord must win the battle of his life. Lord Krishna Himself urges Arjuna to give up all hurry, worry and considerations of right and wrong.

Having given up all hopes, fears and responsibilities, he should seek His refuge alone and He would absolve him of all sins, troubles and tortures. That is why Sanjay concludes the Gita, by saying, "Wherever there is Lord Krishna, the Lord of Yoga and wherever there is Arjuna, the wielder of the Gandiva bow, goodness, victory, glory and righteousness do prevail." So, let us seek the company of Lord Krishna.

The blind King Dhritrashtra was eager to know what was happening on the battle-field. He asked his Charioteer Sanjay to keep on reporting the events taking place on the war front.

Sanjay started reporting thus, "Having seen the Pandava army arrayed on the battle-field, your son Duryodhana approached Dronacharya and asked him to have a glance at the Pandava forces." Bhishma addressed the Princes under his command thus, "A glorious opportunity awaits you.

The gates of heaven are wide open before you. Fight with all your might and attain name and fame. It is your moral duty to die on the battle-field. So, do perform your duty with joy."

Yudhishthira issued orders to Arjuna, "The enemy has a huge force at his disposal. Our army is not so large. Follow the tactics of concentration. Array the army in the needle formation."

Arjuna said to Lord Krishna, "Place my chariot between the two armies and keep it there till I have carefully seen with whom I have to fight in this battle."

Lord Krishna had to yield to the wishes of His devotee who was going to play a pivotal role in this battle for righteousness. He, immediately, drove the chariot into the 'no man's land.'

The serene and peaceful Himalayan valleys gifted us the Upanishadas which enshrine the ultimate truth and reality. The Gita once again proclaims the same truth and wisdom amidst the din and noise of a total war. Each one of us has to fight the battle of his own life. The Gita teaches us how to fight this battle successfully without yielding to temptation and dejection. He who gets dejected in the battle of life is doomed to destruction. No escapism and fleeing from the battle in which all of us, are engaged at our own level. Face it boldly and calmly without any headache or heartache. Thus, the message of the Gita is most suited to the modern man who suffers from a number of incurable maladies, repressions and suppressions which are consuming and killing him day in and out. Here is a certain cure for the so-callled incurables of mankind.

The very first Verse (sloka) of the first chapter of the Gita describes Kurukshetra as Dharmakshetra or 'battle of religion' where the Kaurva and Pandava forces are arrayed against each other to fight. This description is highly symbolic. In fact, this human body or the human heart is the battle-field where in the Mahabharta war is being fought between the forces of good and evil, residing in every bosom.

The Kaurvas are one hundred in number. They stand for the evil forces in man's heart. The Pandavas who are only five in number, represent the diviner impulses in man. They stand for the forces of goodness which are only a few but the victory always belongs to them. We know that truth alone triumphs and not falsehood, as it happened in the hoary past in the case of Lord Rama who vanquished Ravana, the Demon King of Lanka.

A constant Mahabharta war is being waged in every one of us, at all our crucial moments of actions. The negative forces like the Kaurvas in each one of us are larger in number and mightier in their effectiveness. But the divine army within, like the Pandavas, is ever fewer in number and weaker in efficiency. Any single individual at the moment of his inward checking up, finds himself in the grip of grief and dejection as was the case with Arjuna on the battle-field of Kurukshetra.

Thus, most of us resemble Arjuna while performing our duty. The Lord in the Gita talks to us to lift ourselves up from the ditch of depression into which we have fallen because of our wrong notions and identifications.

How relevant is the Gita to the modern man is clearly shown at every step. Think of Arjuna's chariot, driven by Lord Krishna. Verily, the human body is the chariot. It is pulled forward by the five steeds or horses which are our sense-organs—the ears, the skin, the eyes, the tongue, the nostrils. These are the five senses of knowledge which enable a man to hear, to touch, to see, to taste and to smell. It is the mind of man which directs and dictates these sense-organs to work in their respective fields. So, mind is the rein which controls the lusty steeds of the senses.

If we entrust this rein of the mind in the hands of our discriminative intellect or the higher self in us represented by Lord Krishna, we are bound to be victorious in the battle of our life, as Arjuna was a Victor in the battle of Mahabharta.

The Gita, the Divine song, begins with the word, 'Religion' and ends with the word 'Mama' meaning 'Mine.' Thus, the Gita is nothing but the exposition and explanation of My Religion which should not be translated as religion. There is a world of difference between 'Dharma' of Sanskrit and 'Religion' of English.

'Dharma' is derived from the root "Dhri" which means to uphold, sustain and support. It means, "The Law of being' implying, "That which makes a thing or being what it is." For example, it is the Religion of fire to burn. That is why Swami Vivekananda defines religion as 'Being and becoming." Thus 'Religion' means the essential nature of a being or thing.

If we are to live as truly dynamic men in the world, we must live faithfully to our true nature. The Gita is there to explain to me my Religion. If I discover my Religion and act accordingly, I can live in the abiding peace and prosperity on this earth.

Dhritrashtra questions Sanjay, "Gathered on the sacred field of Kururkshetra, eager to fight, what did my sons and the sons of Pandu do ?"

Sanjay narrates to the blind King, the events taking place on the battle-field. Sanjay is endowed with divine vision, as his heart is pure.

There is a short account of the Principal warriors on the Pandava side, such as Satyaki, Virata, Drupada, Dhrstaketu, Kashiraja, Purujit, Kuntibhoja, Saiba, Yudhamanyu, Uttamauja, Abhimanyu and the like.

The Chief warriors on the Kaurva side are : Dronacharya, Bhishma, Karna, Kripacharya, Asvatthama, Vikarna, Bhurishrava and so on.

Duryodhana praises his own army and requests that all should protect Bhishma.

Then, all of a sudden, conchs, kettle-drums, trumpets and horns blared forth. That sound, on the battle-field was tumultuous.

Arjuna requests Lord Krishna to drive forth his chariot between the two armies so that he may behold with whom he is going to fight.

Seeing all his kith and kin and relatives arrayed against him on the battle-field, Arjuna, fearing their destruction, is filled with deep sorrow and grief.

He recounts the evil consequences of destruction of the race and family traditions and of an intermixture of castes. Overwhelmed with despondency, Arjuna lays aside his bow and arrows and tells Krishna that he will not fight.

Arjuna's refusal to fight the battle of his life, has given us the immortal 'Song Divine' or the Bhagavad Gita which is enshrined in millions of hearts as the Word of God. Millions of men all over the world have sought inspiration from this Supreme treasure of human literature.

Patriots kissed the gallows cheerfully, lost in the thoughts of the immortality of the soul. Devotion to duty without any desire for reward confers greatest happiness on mankind. The Gita gives us a view as well as a way of life. It reminds us again and again that we are immortal and not the perishable bodies.

Thus, in the Upanishada, sung by the Lord, the science of Brahma, the scripture of Yoga, the dialogue between Shri Krishna and Arjuna, ends the first chapter entitled "the Yoga of Dejection of Arjuna."

Let us ponder over the significance of these words used at the end of each chapter in the Gita. Each chapter in the Gita is considered as an Upanishada.

So, there are eighteen chapters, say, Upanishadas in this Divine Song. Upanishada is word indicating a literature that is to be studied by sitting (shad), near (Upa) a teacher, in a spirit of receptive meekness and surrender (ni). It teaches us the changeless reality behind the ever-changing world of perceptions and feelings. This great Advaitic truth is termed by the name of Brahman. The word 'Yoga' means to join. The Gita joins us with the Supreme Reality which has no beginning and end. That is why the Gita has been called "Yoga Shastra."

# 6. "SANKHYA YOGA" OR THE YOGA OF KNOWLEDGE

This chapter contains 72 Verses in which we get a summary of the whole philosophical contents of the Gita. The first ten Verses explain the circumstances under which Arjuna totally surrenders to the "Krishna-influence."

The Yoga of knowledge is explained in the Verses 11 to 30. The duty of a man of the warrior class has been described in the Verses 31 to 38. If Arjuna refuses to fight this righteous war, he will be shirking his duty as a warrior. He will lose his reputation and incur sin.

Karmayoga or the Yoga of Selfless Action has been described and explained in the Verses 39 to 53.

In the Verses commencing from 54 and ending with 72, the attributes of the man of stable mind and his glories have been described. The path of love (Bhakti Yoga) and the path of Renunciation have also been indicated in these Verses. A grand synthesis has been attempted as all the paths lead to Him alone. There should be no conflict and confusion about them.

We must bear in mind that the Gita is the greatest philosophical poem of the world. **This Song Divine is being sung in every heart ceaselessly, but we have no ears to listen to it. The ears and all other senses need to be tuned to catch the divine message being delivered within our own bosoms.**

A great symbolism goes on in the Gita in almost every Verse. It conveys a deeper message than what it seems to deliver in a literal sense. That is why the message of the Gita is ever new, fresh, invigorating, cosmopolitan and universal in its appeal and import.

Some people fail to understand how such a long discourse or dialogue could have taken place on the battle-field where the two armies were ready to pounce upon and kill each other at any moment. They are justified to ask how seven hundred Verses could have been spoken and heard in the confused and fearful atmosphere of the war.

The fact is that the message or the preaching given in the Gita belongs undoubtedly to Lord Krishna, but His message has been conveyed to mankind in so many Verses or Slokas by the poet-philosopher Vyasa who was a great seer of mighty intellect and widest sympathies.

Vyasa who was supremely divine held the entire Universe of living beings in his embrace of love. But for him, the Vedas, the Puranas, the Mahabharata and the Gita would not have seen the light of day.

So, out of his love for humanity, he explained the message of Krishna to Arjuna in so many Verses so that all kinds of mind could understand and assimilate it. Thus, the Gita contains Krishna's message and Vyasa's poetry.

Now, first of all, we should try to grasp the deep meaning of Arjuna's surrender to Lord Krishna. An Eternal Truth can be discovered in this sort of surrender. When the ego (Arjuna) in its dejections sits back in the body (chariot), throwing up all instruments of activities (Gandiva) and when the sense-organs (the white horses) are held back well under control by pulling the reins (the mind), the charioteer (the Pure Intellect) shall guide the ego to divine strength.

This divine strength will lead to ultimate success over the greater and mightier forces of evil with the help of a fewer forces of goodness gathered in the very bosom of the seeker.

Understood in this light, the Gita embraces the whole mankind.

Truth is one but the Sages call it by different names. There is no doubt that Truth alone triumphs and not falsehood, as it has been proved by the experience of mankind over the ages.

## 7. WHAT IS THE YOGA OF KNOWLEDGE ?

*"Nothing is more purifying than knowledge"* is the view of Lord Krishna in the Gita. Yoga means to join oneself with the supreme Truth, supreme Consciousness and Bliss. A *real knowledge of the self is realization of God within one's own bosom. The whole animate* and inanimate creation is Brahma or God and that God is my own self.

So, Lord Krishna advises, dejected and grief-stricken Arjuna in these words, "The wise men do not grieve over the dead. There was never a time when I was not present or when you or these Kings were not. We shall never cease to be. Boyhood, youth, old age and death belong to the body and not to the soul. Heat and cold, pleasure and pain are transitory and fleeting and they too belong to the body and mind. The wise man who is not tormented by these contacts of the senses is fit for attaining immortality. The seers of truth know that all these bodies, belonging to the eternal and imperishable soul are perishable. Verily, they are, already, dead and lifeless but seem to be alive because of their contact with the ever-lasting soul. Moreover, the soul neither kills nor it is killed. It is never born; so, it never dies. That is why it is eternal. Weapons cannot cut it, fire cannot burn it, water cannot drench it and wind cannot dry it up. This soul is omnipotent. It is immutable.

Arjuna, this soul dwelling in the bodies of all creatures and human beings can never be slain. Therefore, you need not mourn for anyone. The body is born and it must die sooner or later. So, stand up and fight to do your duty."

Thus, the Path of Knowledge makes a man realise that he is a "soul with a body." The moment True Knowledge about his eternal soul dawns upon a man, all his sufferings and imperfections are over in the twinkling of an eye. It is this Divine Knowledge about the soul known as *Bmhma-Vidya* which delivers us from all bondage. Man awakened to his soul's glory is God, while God forgotten of His own glory is the deluded man of misery. It is our ignorance of our real self which is the root cause of all our ills and ailments. So, know 'thyself' and be free for ever. He who knows himself to be neither the body, nor the mind nor the intellect but the eternal and everlasting soul, becomes God Himself. This is the essence of the Yoga of Knowledge.

## 8. SCIENTIFIC BASIS OF THE SOCIAL SYSTEM

As a warrior too, Arjuna must not flee the battle-field which is perfectly suited to his mental make-up of a Kshatriya. It must be noted here that

Kshatriya is not merely the name of a caste, as it is generally believed by the common man. It is actually the mental trait of an individual. To begin with, the so-called caste system was perfectly scientific in its approach. It was based upon physical, mental and intellectual abilities of persons concerned. Birth alone was not the deciding factor but worth of an individual was to decide whether he should be called a *Brahman or a Vaishya or a shudra or a Kshatriya. A learned man interested in more learning* and teaching was called a Brahman. A person who was interested in serving others was called a Shudra. He who knew the secrets of trade and agriculture was called a Vaishya or a trader. He was interested in the worldly possessions from the core of his heart. Similarly, a Kshatriya was one who could defend the weak, the innocent and the poor. He was the man with the mission of eliminating exploitation, injustice, tyranny, torture and crimes from society. Thus, a caste meant a specific character of the person concerned. One could change his caste by changing his character through tireless efforts. Vishwamitra who was a Kshatriya became a Brahma Rishi like Vashishtha by performing so many austerities. So, how scientific and judicious was the classification of man on the basis of his entire character and characteristics in the days gone by.

Krishna simply reminds his friend Arjuna that by character he is every inch a soldier and a warrior. He should not shirk his duty to fight the enemy who is wedded to evil. In fact, everybody has to act in life, according to his essential nature or character. None can go contrary to his nature.

## 9. CHOICE OF ONE'S OWN BATTLE-FIELD

Thus, it is the desire that leads a man astray. Arjuna, the greatest archer and warrior of his times, desires to become a recluse (sanyasi). He desires to become a beggar although he has the prowess and strength to kill all his foes who have deprived him of all his wealth and kingdom in a deceitful way. Desire has blinded him to his real character or Religion. His ignorance of his real nature is urging him to run away from the battle-field of his life. The battle-field is not peculiar to Arjuna alone. Each one of us has been allotted a battle-field of our own to act. It is nothing but the field of our duty. If I am a man of learning and love knowledge above everything else, my battlefield is confined to books, schools, colleges, students, debates, discussions, reading, writing, preaching and the like. I cannot and should not go to the cricket-field as a batsman to get my head struck with a bouncer. So, Lord Krishna through the medium of his friend Arjuna, is advising man as such to discover his inner real nature before he enters the battle-field of his life.

One should decide one's profession in life, according to one's nature. Then alone, one's efforts will be crowned with grand success. How scientific and modern Krishna is in his analysis of mankind and people's duties ! Moreover, Krishna is not only a friend to Arjuna, but he is a never-failing friend to all of us also. Let us also befriend Him for our welfare and emancipation. What a Universal Guide Krishna is ! The Gita is so relevant to modern man that it provides solutions to all his complex problems of head and heart.

## 10. NO RUNNING AWAY FROM THE WORLD

The Gita does not teach escapism or running away from the challenges of life into some peaceful cave of the Himalayas. Arjuna is willing to do so. He is interested in shirking his duty as a warrior, as most of us are inclined to do. But Krishna insists that he must do his duty at every cost, come what may. There is no escape from duty for anybody in this world. Your inner nature will catch hold of you and force you into action, suited to your special temperament. Lord Krishna advises everybody to do his duty for a number of sound and solid reasons. In fact, every person should put aside his foolish desires and act according to his inner and inherent tendencies or nature.

## 11. HOW TO LIVE IN THIS WORLD

Lord Krishna inspires every body or Arjuna to do his duty, "Nothing is more welcome for a man of the warrior class than a righteous war. If you shirk your duty to fight, you will lose your reputation and incur sin as well. To a hero of fame like you, dishonour is worse than death.

If you die fighting, you will win heaven for yourself. If you conquer, you will enjoy sovereignty of the Earth. Treating alike victory and defeat, gain and loss, pleasure and pain, Arjuna should get ready to fight."

## 12. DESIRE DEGRADES YOU.

It is our desire that invites all our worries, agonies, and hellish turmoil. That is why Lord Krishna lays the greatest stress on Action throughout the Gita. It is known as Karmayoga or the Yoga of selfless Action. Desirelessness alone will enable us to realise the divinity, dwelling in our bosoms and pervading in the whole Universe. Desire prevents us from seeing the soul or God within and without. A pauper who desires nothing is virtually a Prince. A Prince who hankers after more and more riches is nothing but a beggar.

# 13. WORLDLY DESIRES OBLITERATE THE BLISS WITHIN.

Man is the eldest Prince or son of God because God created man in His own image. Man is the very embodiment of Truth (sat), Knowledge (chit) and Bliss (Anand) which are the three attributes of God. This imperishable soul within us is not different from God. It is like a drop in the ocean. When the drop merges with the ocean, it becomes the ocean itself as it is an integral part of the ocean. What prevents man to merge with God ? His own desires, born out of his own ignorance of his True Nature, degrade man from his divinity.

Desires not only delude Arjuna but all of us alike. Arjuna desires not to kill his kith and kin and relatives, although they deserve to be killed and they are desirous of killing Arjuna himself. Similarly, we desire to possess all the material comforts and luxuries like wealth, land, buildings, cars, five star hotels and so on. We think that these lifeless and inanimate objects can cheer up our animate and everlasting soul which is already overflowing with eternal bliss. The dirt of desire tarnishes the mirror of the mind and intellect to reflect the divinity within our bosoms.

So, Krishna advises us to give up our desires and feel happy on our own. His life on the whole is a message of joy and cheer. The flute on his lips signifies his perpetual happiness. "Keep smiling," seems to be Krishna's philosophy, expressed in two words. That is why He cannot see His dear friend Arjuna weeping in life out of sheer ignorance and stupidity. 'Krishna cure' is a panacea to us all. He advises us not to yield to ignorance, desires, stupidity and temptations. Desireless activity will lead us to self-realization and bliss.

# 14. THE PATH OF ACTION

"Work is worship," is the essence of Karmayoga. Each one of us has to do something or the other in our life. No one can live without work even for a moment. The Karmayoga is the technique of doing our duty in life with such an attitude of mind as will unite us with the Supreme Spirit or Godhood. Self-realisation is possible even by a man of action who does his duty as a devotion to God, without any selfish motive.

Through Karma (action), a man can grow and fulfil his evolution to identify himself with his own Real Nature—the Self. Single-pointed Karma without desire for the fruits shall bring about inner purification which is a necessary condition for the spiritual awakening.

Karmayoga is the art of living and acting in a disciplined spirit supported by the Divine inspiration. Lord Krishna tells Arjuna, "Thy right is to work only. But never covet for its fruits; let not the fruit of action be thy motive, nor let thy attachment lead to inaction. Perform action, O Dhananjaya, being steadfast in Yoga, abandoning attachment and balanced in success and failure. Evenness of mind is called Yoga."

A complete technique of how one can live the life of a truly inspired worker is explained here. A true worker should act in the world established in equipoise and equanimity or evenness of mind undisturbed, by ups and downs, success or failures, pleasure or pain. He must renounce his attachment as well because it is the main factor behind all his sorrows and sufferings. The fruit of action is there in the future. If a student is constantly worried about his marks in the annual examination, he will not be able to put his heart and soul into his studies right now in the present. He will be living in the future without studying hard in the present with single-minded devotion and dedication.

The future is not yet born. It is the proper use of the present moments that makes the future glorious. Let us not waste our energies in worrying about the fruits of action in future. The desire-prompted activities thicken the veil of ignorance while a desireless activity tears this veil of ignorance in due course of time. Unselfish work performed in a spirit of dedication and egoless surrender is the secret method of exhausting our passions for worldly things. When the mind is purified through Karmayoga, the Eternal Godhood is discovered by man. Thus, Gyan Yoga and Karma Yoga or the Yoga of knowledge and the Yoga of Action lead to the same goal of Godhood. One has to choose between the two according to one's mental traits.

## 15. TRAITS OF A MAN OF STABLE MIND

Arjuna is eager to know the qualities of a man of steady wisdom. Lord Krishna describes such a perfect man in these words, "He whose mind is not shaken by adversity, who does not hanker after pleasures, who is free from attachment, fear and anger is called a sage of steady wisdom. He is the master of his senses. That which is night to all beings, in that state of Divine knowledge and supreme bliss, the God-realized sage keeps awake. When the ignorant are awake in their sense-life, it is a night to the seer. As the waters of different rivers enter the ocean; which though full on all sides remains undisturbed; likewise, he, in whom all enjoyments merge themselves attains peace; not he who hankers after such enjoyments. He who has given up all desires and moves free from attachment, egoism and thirst for enjoyment attains peace."

Perfection or self-realization can be attained by reaching a state of desirelessness through the practice of either the Yoga of knowledge or the Yoga of Action or the Yoga of devotion or all the three taken together. The Truth is one but the sages call it by different names. These petty but pretty mundane desires to gain the power and pelf in the world will evaporate the moment, a person dives deep into the very ocean of Eternal Bliss, surging in his own bosom.

# 16. "KARMAYOGA" OR THE YOGA OF ACTION

Arjuna is eager to know which path he should follow for his self-development. We too are interested in knowing whether we should follow the path of Knowledge or the path of Action so that we may have the vision of the Absolute Truth or Godhood in this very life.

There is no scope for blind faith in the Vedanta or in the Gita. There is an intimate and free discussion between the teacher and the taught. No other religion in the world allows so much freedom for the disciple. But in the Gita, Arjuna is completely free to ask openly, contradict and argue with Lord Krishna whatever comes to his mind. Just see the patience of Lord Krishna. He never gets annoyed with his friend Arjuna. This is the hallmark of a great teacher who keeps on loving his student, in spite of his colossal ignorance. That is why Krishna has been declared to be the Universal teacher of the whole world.

What is the path to perfection ? According to Shankaracharya, action and renunciation are advised in the Vedas for a seeker of perfection. Indeed, no living creature endowed with intelligence and mind can remain even for a moment without doing some work or the other. Cessation of all activities is the signature of death. So, we must act from birth to death. The crucial question is how to act. What is the path of Right Action. He who knows this path and treads upon it reaches the Supreme Ocean of Bliss just like a river falling spontaneously into the Ocean. God-dedicated selfless action performed in a spirit of devotion and self-surrender leads one to the ultimate destination.

We may call it work without attachment or action without desiring any fruit. Work for work's sake, is the secret revealed by the Lord to his dear friend Arjuna on the battle-field of life. If a student studies for study's sake, he is bound to become a great scholar sooner or later. He shall be a genius. He may shatter all the previous records of the Board or the University. There is no limit to his intellectual achievements. But if he studies merely to get through the examination by cramming cheap notes and guides, what will be his mental calibre ? He will remain a backward child.

The moment we work with the motive or desire of getting a reward, efficiency in work is lost. Excellence and perfection in work can never be achieved if the target is to grab a particular fruit or reward for the work done. Our work shall be limited by the expected reward. It can never go beyond it. Our world has changed out of recognition by means of the scientific inventions during the last 250 years. How did the inventors of steam engine, the aeroplane, the wireless, the internal combustion engine and the electricity work ?

Were they motivated by some reward in the form of gold, name or fame ? Certainly not. No fruit or reward or profit was there in their minds when they were lost in their work of inventing new things with which their minds were fired. They were unmindful even of their bodies. They forgot even their thirst and hunger. Their wives and mothers brought food for them in their laboratories. They asked them to put the food there and go away. When the mother rerturned after six hours to inquire, the scientist (Marconi) replied that he had eaten it. But the mother found the whole food in the dish untouched ! This is the secret of work or the path of selfless action which Lord Krishna is explaining to Arjuna, "Do your duty whole-heartedly."

If the secret of work or Karmyoga is properly understood and digested, a player will become a better player, a teacher will become a better teacher, a doctor will become a better doctor, a cook will become a better cook and a warrior shall shine forth the mightiest one as happens in the case of Arjuna. Verily, mind is the man. When the mind is perplexed and puzzled and tossed with confusing desires, it cannot function efficiently. But when it works for the sake of work with single-pointed devotion, it can do wonders undreamt of.

## 17. WHEN DOES DEATH BECOME BLESSED ?

Lord Krishna further enlightens Arjuna by saying, "He who takes delight in the self alone and is gratified with the self and is contented in the self, has no duty. Therefore, go on doing your duty efficiently without attachment. There is nothing in all the three worlds for Me to do, yet I continue to work to maintain the three worlds. As the unwise act with attachment, the wise should act without attachment. Man should never allow himself to be swayed by attraction and repulsion. Even death in the performance of one's own duty brings blessedness."

Death becomes a boon only when a person breathes his last in the awareness of the immortality of his soul. He must not die in a swoon, unaware of the eternal spark of life within. He should be able to see his body falling inch by inch. The spirit within must see that the senses are failing or dying one by one by slow degrees. Just as we feel the death of our childhood and youth in our old age without any grief; so also while departing from the body, we should stand apart from the body, as we stand apart from our clothes. The everlasting conscious soul should visualize that it is withdrawing itself from the garments of the body, mind and intellect which are merely the matter envelopments of the superconscious soul. He who dies in such an awareness becomes immortal as he merges with the Supreme Reality like the drop of water, falling into the ocean to become the ocean itself.

## 18. WHAT PROMPTS MAN TO COMMIT SIN ?

Arjuna asks Krishna a very crucial question, "What is it that forces a man to commit sin much against his will ?"

The Lord replies, "It is the desire, born of ignorance which is the root cause of all sins and evils. Know this desire to be insatiable. This desire dwells in the senses, the mind and the intellect. Anger crops up if the desires remain unfulfilled. Greed crops up if they are fulfilled.

Thus, desires throw a man into the trap of anger and greed which lead to hell. So, dear Arjuna, you must control the desire to live in perpetual peace and bliss."

In fact, it is the passion or desire which is at the root of all sins. It is the flesh that desires so many things but the soul desires nothing. So, be seated in the soul.

## 19. ETERNITY OF THE SOUL

Inspired by a divine remembrance, Lord Krishna declares that He Himself preached the Vedas to the Sun at the beginning of the Creation. Later on, the Sun-God preached to his son, Manu, the ancient Law Giver of India. Manu, in his turn passed it on to Ikshvaku, the ancestor of the Solar Dynasty who ruled over Ayodhya for a long period of time.

The idea that the Vedas are eternal cannot be easily digested by a modern student. But, here, by the Vedas, we do not mean the Vedic 'text books' which are, no doubt, perishable. When we speak of the "Vedas", we mean the 'knowledge of the Divine Spark within and without'. So, the Divine nature of man is indeed eternal. Krishna tells Arjuna that there was never a time in the entire past when they were not there or those Kings and princes or warriors were not there, as the soul never ceases to be. Goswami Tulsidas mentions in his immortal work 'Ramcharitmanas' that this imperishable and eternal soul keeps on wandering in eighty four lakhs of manifestations (*yonies*) before it assumes the human form.

Here it must be noted that the word (Veda) is derived from the root 'Vid' which means 'to know'. Therefore, 'Veda' means the knowledge of the divinity, lurking in man and the technique by which it can be brought out to full manifestation.

Modern science accepts the fact that the creation of the Universe must have started with the Sun. When Lord Krishna tells Arjuna that He Himself gave this divine knowledge of the self to the Sun, it means that this knowledge is as eternal and immortal as the soul itself.

## 20. NO FALL TO A MAN OF FAITH

Arjuna asks Krishna, "What becomes of the soul of the person who is endowed with faith but has not been able to subdue his passions and whose mind is diverted from Yoga or God-Realization at the time of death ?"

The Lord replies, "Dear Arjuna, there is no fall for him either here or hereafter. He who strives for self-redemption or God-Realization never meets with evil destiny. He who has fallen from Yoga obtains the higher worlds of heaven to which men of virtuous deeds alone have entry. Having resided there for countless years, he takes birth in the house of some pious and wealthy man. If he is possessed of dispassion, he is born in the family of enlightened Yogis. But such a birth in the world is very difficult to attain. He regains easily the spiritual insight of his previous birth. Slowly but steadily, he follows the path of God-Realization and attains perfection in the end."

## 21. OMNI-PRESENCE OF GOD

The Blessed Lord further enlightens Arjuna and says, "O Dhananjaya ! I am the source of the whole Universe. There is nothing else besides Me, Arjuna. All this is strung on Me, as clusters of gems on a string."

"I am the sapidity in water, O son of Kunti. I am the light in the Moon and the Sun. I am the syllable OM in all the Vedas, sound in ether and the manliness in men. I am the sweet fragrance in the Earth and the brilliance in fire. I am the life in all beings. I am austerity in men of ascetics."

"Know Me, O Partha, as the eternal seed of all beings. I am the intelligence of the intelligent; the glory of the glorious. Arjuna, of the mighty, I am the might, free from passion and desire; in beings I am the sexual desire, not conflicting with virtue or scriptural injunctions."

## 22. FREEDOM FROM BIRTH AND DEATH

Having attained the human birth by the grace of the Lord, he who does not realize his divine nature, comes into the womb of mother again and again. He suffers countless agonies of constant births and deaths. It is mentioned in the scriptures that a dying man experiences pangs of being stung by a thousand scorpions or snakes all at once. Pangs of birth are equally horrible.

Childhood is somewhat free from worries. But when the child grows up into an adult or a youth, countless desires of sex, name, fame, education, power and pelf start consuming him day in and day out. He knows neither rest nor peace of mind. The moment one desire is satisfied, another crops up in a never-ending vicious circle. In due course of time, old age pounces upon him like a tiger. Physical strength and senses fail him. He trembles, as he tries to walk. His unfulfilled desires and passions tear him to pieces.

Broken hearted and despised by all his kith and kin, sons, daughters and wife, he breathes his last in great agony and is born again to fulfil his unfulfilled desires. The cycle is once again pedalled. He keeps on pedalling it till he realizes the immortality of his blissful soul. The Gita can rescue him from the cycle of births and deaths.

## 23. THE PRINCIPLE OF THE TRANSMIGRATION OF THE SOUL

Krishna is now ready to declare the greatest secret to his dear friend, Arjuna. The Blessed Lord says, "The worshippers of the Gods go to the gods. The worshippers of the ancestors go to the ancestors.

Those who adore the spirits or ghosts, reach the spirits. But those who worship Me come to Me alone. That is why My devotees are no longer subject to birth and death. They merge in Me."

Arjuna throws a query to Krishna, "O Master of Yoga, through what process of continuous meditation shall I know you ? In what particular forms, O Lord, are you to be meditated upon by me ?"

## 24. UNIVERSAL VISION OF GOD

Krishna replies, giving a glimpse of his unlimited divine glories, "Arjuna, I am the Universal Self, seated in the heart of all beings. I alone, am the beginning, the middle and also the end of all beings. I am Vishnu among twelve sons of Aditi and the radiant Sun among the luminaries.

I am the glow of the Maruts who are the forty-nine wind-gods. I am also the Moon among the stars. Among the Vedas, I am the Sam Veda, among the gods, I am Indra. I am the mind among the organs of perception. I am the life-energy in all beings. I am Shiva among the eleven Rudras who are gods of destruction. Among the great seers, I am Bhrigu.

Among words, I am the sacred syllable OM. Among all trees, I am the Pipal-tree and among the perfected ones, I am Muni Kapila. Know Me among horses as Ucchaisravas, born of Amrita, among lordly elephants, the Airavata and among men, the King. Among cows, I am the celestial cow Kamdhenu, the cow of plenty. Among serpents, I am Vasuki. Among controllers, I am Yama, the God of Death. Among beasts, I am the lion and among birds, I am Garuda."

Arjuna prays to Krishna, "I desire to see your Divine Form, possessed of wisdom, glory, energy, strength, valour and effulgence, O Mighty Lord !"

The Blessed Lord says, "O Partha ! behold my Divine Cosmic Form of various colours and shapes. Behold in Me, the twelve sons of Aditi, the eight Vasus, the eleven Rudras, the two Aswin Kumars and the Maruts and many more wonderful forms never seen before."

But Lord Krishna warns Arjuna, "You cannot see Me with these eyes of yours. So, I give thee (you) the Vision Divine." Much confusion surrounds this concept of Vision Divine or the 'Divine Eye.' It must be clarified. The intellectual comprehension is meant here by the term 'Seeing' and the capacity of the intellect to comprehend is the 'Divine Eye.' So, I do not believe that Krishna transformed Himself into His Cosmic Form, but He only helped Arjuna to gain the necessary inward adjustments so that he might see what was already there in Krishna. It is extremely necessary to peep through the symbolism in the Verses of the Gita. It is the right understanding alone that can deliver us from all kinds of bondage.

To see "the one in the many" is the work of a heart full of staunch faith. But to see "the many in the one", we, not only need the heart, but an educated intellect also. The ordinary can be seen by the bodily eyes. But the extraordinary or the supernatural can be seen only by the 'vision of the intellect'.

# 25. SIGNIFICANCE OF THE FOUR-HANDED VISHNU

Arjuna declares, "I see Thee with 'Crown, Club and Discus' a mass of radiance shining everywhere, very hard to look at, all round blazing like burning fire and the Sun and immeasurable on all sides."

Let us ponder over the above-mentioned description of the Lord in detail. The four-handed Vishnu carries in His Hands, the Conch, the Discus, the Club and the Lotus. This is extremely symbolical and has a deep meaning to be understood by one and all. The Lotus represents peace and joy and detachment. The Conch blows and calls man to duty. If there happens to be a generation that does not listen to the higher call in themselves, they are visited by restlessness, war, pestilence, famine, storms and chaotic social and communal disturbances.

If they do not give up their evil ways, despite suffering these maladies, the Club comes down to smother the generation to shape and discipline. Even after this punishment, if there be a generation so totally dissipated that it cannot improve, the Discus, the sharp toothed wheel, 'Sudarshan-Chakra' ever-revolving, the Whirling Weapon of Time comes into operation.

From the Universal Form of Krishna, seen by Arjuna, it becomes clear that the same Truth is the Substratum, not only to the lowest of the low worms, but even to the Trinity. The eternal Truth is one and the same everywhere at all times. But the manifestations are varied and different.

# 26. THE ETERNAL TREE OF CREATION

Lord Krishna further tells Arjuna that this Universe is like a Peepal tree which has emanated from the Almighty God, the Lord of Disillusionment. Unlike other trees, this tree of the Universe has its roots above as it has sprung from God.

During the evolution of this tree of creation, Brahma or the Creator appears, first of all.

Hence, it is Brahma who represents its stem. The abode of Brahma is situated in a lower plane as his rank is lower than that of the Lord. The Vedas which have flowed from Brahma are the leaves of this tree.

Fed by the three Traits and having sense-objects for their tender leaves, the branches of this tree in the shape of the different forms of creation extend both downwards and upwards.

The roots of this tree which bind the soul according to its actions in the human body, are spread in all regions.

This Tree of Creation has no stability. It is in a state of constant flux. What it was a moment ago, it ceases to be the very next moment. This Tree of Creation cannot be felled unless we give up the feelings of 'I' and 'mine' as well as our latent desires.

Arjuna inquires of Krishna, "Those who, endowed with faith, worship gods and others, casting aside the injunctions of the Scriptures, where do they stand? To what nature do they belong—Sattva, Rajas or Tamas?"

Krishna clarifies, "The faith of all men conforms to their mental constitution, Arjuna. Men having sattvika disposition worship gods. Those who have Rajasika temperament worship demi-gods and demons. While others who are men of a Tamsika disposition worship the spirits of the dead and groups of ghosts."

The destiny of these worshippers varies, according to the object of their worship. The worshippers of gods attain celestial bodies. The worshippers of demi-gods and demons are reborn as demi-gods and demons.

While the worshippers of the ghosts or the spirits attain the form, traits and conditions of the ghosts and the spirits. So, one ought to be careful in one's worship. We are bound to become what we worship with the passage of time.

## 27. THE ART OF A GLORIOUS DEATH

Arjuna is eager to know the destiny of the person who dies with the thought of God uppermost in his mind.

Krishna enlightens him by telling him the technique of dying, "Having closed all the doors of the senses and firmly holding the mind in the cavity of the heart and then, fixing the life-breath in the head, remain steadfast in Yogic concentration on God. He who departs from the body, uttering the one indestructible Brahma, OM, reaches the Supreme Goal—The Vishnu's Abode."

## 28. OM—THE SUPREME PATH TO SALVATION

The word 'OM' is an appellation or title of the indestructible Supreme Reality or God. This sacred word should be chanted time and again. The Kathopanishad says about OM, "This indestructible syllable is Brahma, or the Supreme Being. Knowing this very syllable, man is able to attain whatever he may like to have."

One may ask, "How can it be possible for one to utter the word 'OM' when all the senses and the mind have been restrained and withdrawn within ?"

Our answer is that the 'Verse' does not lay stress on vocal utterance. It is the utterance by the mind. It is the mind that leads us to our future birth and incarnation. Mind is the leader. So, let us awaken our mind to attain the 'salvation'.

## 29. ARJUNA ENLIGHTENED

Having taught all the secrets of life and death, Krishna asks Arjuna, "Have you heard this gospel of the Gita with a single-minded devotion ? Has your delusion, born of ignorance melted away, O Mighty Warrior ?"

Arjuna replies thus, "O Lord Krishna ! by your grace, my delusion has fled and wisdom has dawned upon me. All my doubts have gone to the winds. I am seated in myself, I will act upon your bidding." The mighty Arjuna springs up to his feet and the Mahabharata war begins.

## 30. YUDHISHTHIRA SEEKS BENEDICTION

Everybody and everything was ready for the battle to begin. All of a sudden, both the armies were bewildered to see Yudhishthira, the steadfast, taking off his armour and putting aside his weapons descending from his chariot and walking on foot towards the Commander of the Kaurva Forces. Everybody was puzzled at this strange behaviour on the part of the brave son of Pandu.

Arjuna too was perplexed and worried. He jumped down from his chariot to follow Yudhishthira. Bheema, Nakula, Sahdeva and Krishna himself followed suit. They thought that Yudhishthira might have decided to seek peace at any cost. They feared that he was going to surrender before an arrow was shot. In spite of Arjuna's asking, Dharmaputra did not tell him anything but kept on walking towards the enemy lines, lost in deep thought.

Then, Krishna, who knew the hearts of men, spoke out, "He is going to the Grand-Sire Bhishma to seek his blessings. He will bow at the feet of Dronacharya to seek his permission and benediction before commencing this terrible fight. That is why he goes unarmed. He respects his elders. With their blessings, we may win this battle."

The people in Duryodhana's army thought that the eldest Pandava was frightened at their strength. A cowardly person as he was, he was coming to negotiate for peace.

But Yudhishthira went straight to Bhishma, bent low to touch his feet and said, "Grand-Sire, permit us to begin the battle. We know that you are unconquerable and matchless. We seek your blessings before launching this terrible battle."

Bhishma, the Grand-Sire was deeply moved and replied, "Child, I am greatly pleased at your noble conduct. Fight and you shall have victory. Although I am bound to fight on the side of the Kaurvas, yet you shall not be defeated." Then, he went to Guru Drona and touched his feet to seek his blessings. Drona said, "O son of Religion, I am obliged to fight for the Kaurvas. I am a slave to my vested interests. But victory shall be yours."

Having sought the blessings of Kripacharya and uncle Salya, Yudhishthira returned to the Pandava lines. Then, the battle began with single combats between the leading Chiefs who were armed with similar weapons. There was also indiscriminate fighting among ordinary or common soldiers. It was named "Sankula Yudha." A large number of men died fighting. Piles of slaughtered soldiers, elephants and horses lay on the ground which had become a bloody mire in which the chariots could not move about freely.

The Kaurva Forces under Bhishma's command kept on fighting for ten days. Then Dronacharya took over the command. When Drona was killed, it was Karna who commanded the Kaurva Forces. When Karna fell towards the close of the seventeenth day's battle, Salya took over the command on the last day.

# 31. THE FIRST DAY'S BATTLE (THE VALIANT ABHIMANYU)

The first day's battle was a mad and horrible carnage. Horses were neighing, elephants were trumpeting and their 'lion-roars' were uttered by the warriors on both the sides. Arrows flew in the air like the burning missiles. Fathers and sons, uncles and nephews killed one another, forgetting their ties of blood.

Bhishma's chariot was dancing like Shiva, causing wide spread destruction on its path. As a result, the Pandava army was badly shaken. Abhimanyu could not bear this sight. So, he stood in the way of his chariot and attacked the Grand-sire. The youngest and the oldest warriors were face to face with each other. The gods in the heaven came forth to watch this combat.

Abhimanyu hit Bhishma nine times with his sharp shafts. Kritavarma was also hit with one of his arrows. Salya was hit five times with the blazing arrows. Abhimanyu's sword-edge arrow beheaded Durmukha's charioteer whose head rolled on the ground. Kripa's bow was broken by his arrow. His feats of bravery brought down showers of flowers from the gods who were watching him with great interest. Bhishma exclaimed, "What a worthy son to a worthy father !"

The desperate Kaurva warriors launched a combined attack on the valiant Abhimanyu but he stood like a rock against them all. All the arrows shot by Bhishma were parried. He aimed an arrow at the Grand-sire's palm tree flag and brought it down in the twinkling of an eye.

Bhishma was overjoyed at this feat of his brave Great-grand son. He roared like a lion.

In spite of the valour, displayed by Abhimanyu, the Pandava Forces suffered badly on the first day of the battle. King Virata's Son, Uttara was killed by Salya and Sveta, the other son, was killed by Bhishma.

Moreover, thousands of soldiers, horses and elephants were killed.

On the other hand, Duryodhana's joy knew no bounds. Dharmaputra was seized with fear. But Krishna consoled Yudhishthira and exhorted him thus, "Do not fear, as God has blessed you with valiant brothers.

Virata; Drupada, Satyaki and Dhrishtadyumna are there with you, besides myself. Don't get dejected. Do you forget that Shikhandi is awaiting for his pre-destined Victim Bhishma ?"

# 32. THE SECOND DAY'S BATTLE (THE VALIANT ARJUNA)

Bhishma again launched massive attacks on the Pandava forces, breaking their formation and killing them in large numbers.

Arjuna turned to his charioteer Krishna and said, "Our army will soon be destroyed by the Grand-Sire. Unless we slay him, we cannot save our army.

Krishna replied, "Then, get ready. Look ! there is the Grand-Sire's chariot. I am driving straight towards him."

Arjuna's chariot sped forward at a great pace. The Grand-Sire shot arrows at the advancing chariot. Many warriors came forward to prevent Arjuna from reaching the Grand-sire's chariot.

But none could stop him. Arjuna beheaded the warriors who stood in his way of reaching Bhishma. His chariot flashed, hither and thither, killing the soldiers and the warriors on the way.

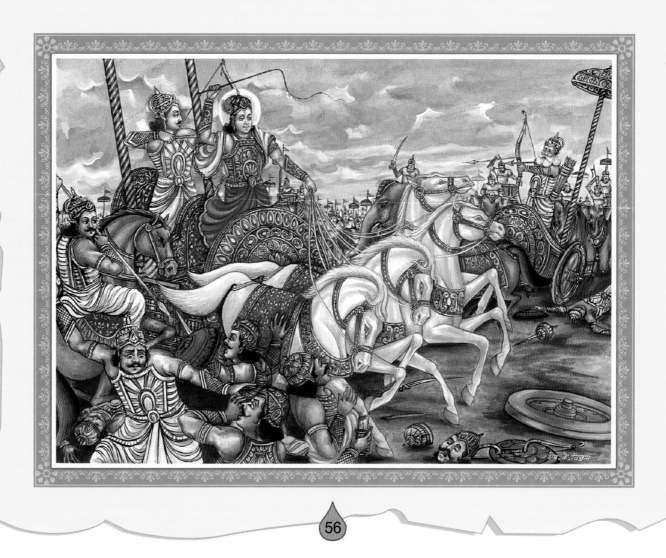

The gods descended from the heavens to watch the combat between Bhishma and his grand-son Arjuna. They were at that time, two of the greatest warriors on the Earth. Their chariots were drawn by white steeds. Arrows in large numbers flew from either side. Shafts met in the air. Every, now and then, the arrows shot by Bhishma hit Arjuna's chest and that of Krishna.

The blood flowing from Krishna's chest enhanced His glory and splendour. Arjuna was beside himself with rage when he saw his dear charioteer bleeding. He showered arrows with all his might at Bhishma. The battle raged for a long time, as both were of equal strength and stamina.

Drona and his sworn enemy Dhrishtadyumna, Draupadi's brother, fought fiercely, in another part of the battle-field. Bheema moved among his enemies like death itself. He felled them to the ground in great numbers. Bhishma's horse bolted carrying him away from the battle-field. The Pandava Army was wild with joy.

The Kaurva Army suffered great losses. Its soldiers were weary and disheartened. At the end of second day's battle, the Kaurvas were depressed and dejected. Dhananjaya and others returned to their camp in great cheer. The day belonged to them.

On the third day, Bhishma had arrayed his army in the 'eagle formation'. The Pandavas had a 'crescent formation' of their army.

As soon as, the battle began, blood began to flow in torrents. The dust that rose from the movements hid the Sun. Arjuna's chariot was covered with shafts like a great cloud of locusts. But Arjuna retaliated by raising a moving fortification of arrows, shot from his Gandiva, around his chariot to protect himself.

Bheema and his son Ghatotkacha displayed remarkable valour in attacking Duryodhana and his men, Consequently, Duryodhana fell in a swoon in his chariot.

Then, the Grand-Sire Bhishma resumed his operations with all his might and main. The Pandavas thought as if the Grand-Sire were fighting at several fronts.

So swift were his movements that he was seen everywhere in the battle-field. Krishna, at this juncture, exhorted Arjuna to get ready to kill Bhishma; otherwise, the whole of the Pandava Army would be killed by the Grand-Sire that afternoon.

"Drive on," said Arjuna.

Now, Arjuna's chariot was speeding on to Bhishma who welcomed it with his sharp shafts. Arjuna broke Bhishma's bow. The moment he picked up another bow, it too was broken by Dhananjaya. The Grand-Sire's heart was gladdened to see Arjuna's skill in archery.

But the Grand-Sire caused havoc when he picked up his third bow. Arjuna faltered with his bow. Krishna's fury was aroused when he realised that the Grand-Sire was bent upon killing Arjuna that day.

He dropped the reins. In the twinkling of an eye, Krishna took up his discus and jumped down from the chariot and pounced upon Bhishma.

But Bhishma was not, at all perturbed, as he saw Krishna approaching towards him. His face beamed with unspeakable joy. He was thrilled to see the Lord of the three worlds before him.

Bhishma exclaimed, "Welcome to Thee, Oh Lotus-eyed one, I bow to you, O Krishna. How gracious of you to come down from the chariot for my sake. My life is for you. Take it away and glorify me in the three worlds. Grant me the boon that I die at your hands, so that I join the ranks of the immortal."

Arjuna was distressed to see that Krishna was going to break his pledge for his sake. He ran after Krishna and with great difficulty managed to bring him back to his chariot.

The chariot reins were once again in Krishna's hands. Arjuna launched furious attacks on the Kaurva Forces. He killed them by thousands.

The Kaurvas ran in panic under his severe blows. They took to their heels to save themselves from Arjuna's sharp shafts. But they had already suffered heavy losses in the form of men, horses and elephants.

While returning to their camps in the torch light, the Kaurva soldiers said to one another, "None can equal Arjuna. He is matchless and peerless. It is his birth-right to be victorious."

On the tenth day of the battle, Arjuna, kept Sikhandi in front of him and attacked Bhishma. Shikhandi was born a girl. Bhishma's principles would not permit him to attack a woman. It was below Bhishma's dignity to wield his weapons against a woman. Krishna knew that the Grand-Sire could be killed only when Arjuna shielded himself with Shikhandi in front of him. When Shikhandi's arrows pierced Bhishma's chest, sparks flew from the Grand-Sire's eyes. His anger for a moment rose like furious flames of fire. But the very next moment, he restrained himself knowing that he was face to face with a woman. Moreover, he knew that his end was imminent.

So, he calmed himself down. Arjuna who had now steeled his heart, aimed his sharp and mighty shafts at the weak points in Bhishma's armour. But the Grand-Sire stood still like a statue, as Arjuna was discharging his arrows from behind Sikhandi.

Bhishma smiled, as the arrows kept on piercing into his bosom. He merely exclaimed, "Ah, these are Arjuna's arrows !" With arrows sticking all over his body so densely that not even an inch of space was left in between, Bhishma, the Grand-Sire, fell from his chariot headlong to the ground. No sooner did he fall than the gods folded their hands in reverent salutation.

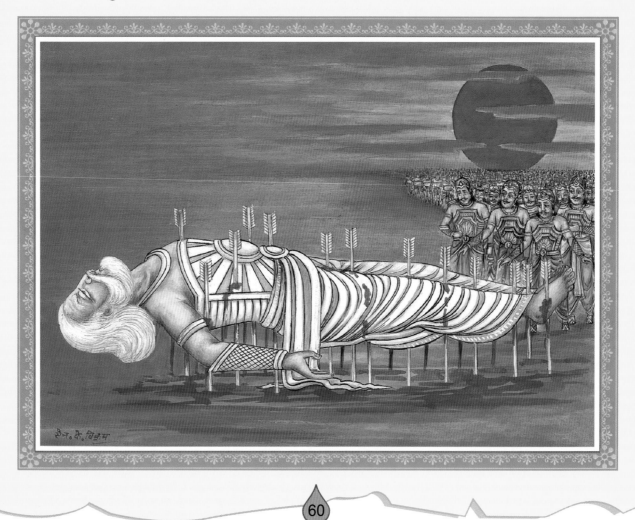

A gentle breeze, laden with fragrant rain drops swept over the battle-field of Mahabharta. Thus, Bhishma, the great son of Ganga who hallowed this Earth fell down. The blameless hero who out of his sweet will remained a celibate for the whole of his life to confer happiness on his father, repaid his debt to Duryodhana. Bhishma was the undefeated bowman. He would not give up his principles come what might. He sanctified the battle-field with his blood. The hearts of the Kaurvas were shocked at Bhishma's downfall. He was a mighty warrior and the most learned man of his times. Since the arrows were sticking out all over his body, Bhishma, as he fell, did not touch the ground. His body was held on the arrows. Fighting ceased. All the warriors came running to where he lay on his bed of arrows. All the Kings stood around him with bowed heads.

The Grand-Sire complained that his head was hanging down unsupported. The Princes and Kings ran and brought pillows to give support to his hanging head. Bhishma rejected them all with a smile and turned his gaze towards Arjuna and exclaimed, "My dear Partha, would you give me a suitable pillow ?" Arjuna at once, knew what the Grand-Sire desired. He took three arrows out of his quiver and placed them under Bhishma's head as a support. Bhishma, then, addressed the assembled warriors, "Arjuna alone knows what I want. My head is, at rest now. I must lie, thus, till the Sun turns north. My soul cannot leave this body till then."

Once again the Grand-Sire looked at Partha and said, "Dear son, thirst is tormenting me. Give me some water to quench my thirst."

Arjuna obeyed. He raised his bow and drawing it to his ear, shot an arrow into the Earth, near Bhishma on his right side. In a moment, there gushed out a stream of pure, cold and sweet water to the very mouth of the Grand-Sire. It is said that the Ganga came up to quench her dear son's tormenting thirst. Having drunk to his fill, Bhishma was delighted on his bed of arrows.

The impure blood generated by impure food bought by the ill-gotten wealth of Duryodhana had tarnished the blood, flowing in Bhishma's veins. Arjuna's sharp shafts stuck in Bhishma's body had spilled that impure blood on the battle-field. Now, true knowledge dawned upon Bhishma. So, he was able to guide Duryodhana.

Bhishma, then, looked at Duryodhana and advised him thus, "Did you see Arjuna's feat in quenching my thirst ? Make peace with him and the Pandavas without any further delay. Put an end to this war, this very moment before I breathe my last. That will save you and others from the impending doom."

But Duryodhana did not relish what the departing Grand-Sire advised him to do. The Grand-Sire's sane advice fell flat on his ears. He turned a deaf ear to what Bhishma had said. He was burning with the fire of revenge. But the arrogant Duryodhana did not know that he was inviting his doom nearer each day. When the hour of destruction comes, the mind and intellect often get perverted. The patient on his death-bed refuses to take the medicine as its taste happens to be bitter. Similar was the case with Duryodhana who was heading fast towards his doom. He was going to meet his nemesis. His position was that of a drowning man who caught at a straw to save himself.

When Karna came to know the fate of Bhishma who lay wounded and dying on the battle-field, he rushed to the place and falling at his feet said, "Most revered Grand-Sire, Radha's son Karna prostrates himself before you."

Bhishma was greatly moved. He tenderly put his hand on Karna's head and blessing him uttered, "My dear young man, you are not Radha's son. But in fact, you are Kunti's own first born son. The omni-scient Narada himself revealed this secret to me. You are the son of the Surya. I never disliked you. You are equal in strength to Arjuna and Krishna. The Pandavas are your brothers. My wish is that you should join them as a brother."

Karna humbly and respectfully replied, "I too know that I am Kunti's son. But I must be true to Duryodhana whose salt I have eaten. It is now impossible for me to cross over to the Pandavas. I must repay the debt with my life. I owe it to Duryodhana for his love and faith in me. Kindly forgive me and bless me, Grand-Sire." Bhishma, the very embodiment of Religion, reflected for a while and replied, "You are right. Do as you wish, as that alone is the right path for you now."

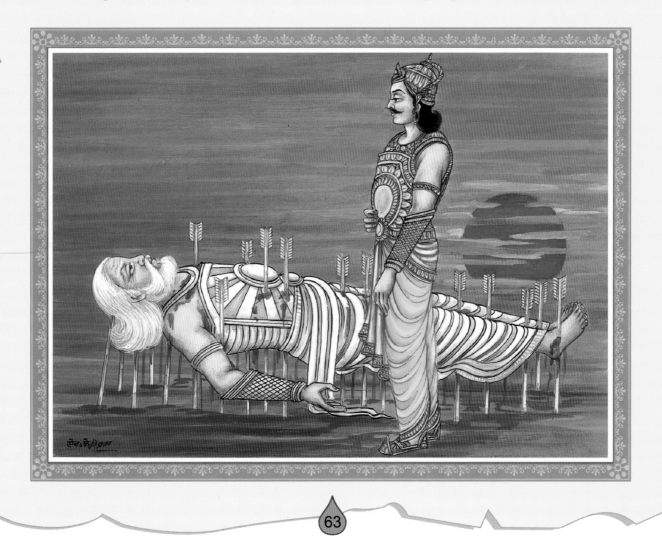

When Karna agreed to lead the Kaurva Forces, he once again went to Bhishma to seek his blessings and saluting him, he addressed, "Peerless Grand-Sire, I have come to you for your gracious blessings, as I am asked to lead the Kaurva Forces after your fall."

Bhishma blessed Karna and said, "You are like rain clouds to living creatures. None can equal you in loyalty and firmness. Serve Duryodhana and be true to your salt. May fortune smile on you !"

When Karna appeared on the battle-field, mounting on his chariot, there was a great jubilation in the Kaurva Forces.

## 36. DRONACHARYA IN SUPREME COMMAND OF THE KAURVA FORCES

Duryodhana consulted his dear friend, Karna, as to who should be appointed the Supreme Commander of the Army. Karna reflected for a while and then said, "Although all the Kings on our side possess almost equal strength, prowess, skill, courage, valour and wisdom, yet we cannot put them all in a joint command. If we choose any one of them, the rest will feel belittled and insulted. It may be fatal to us."

"So, my choice falls on Drona who happens to be the teacher and Guru of them all. If we appoint him as the Supreme Commander, all the warriors will feel honoured and secure ; for none equals him in the art and craft of war-fare. He shall be the fountain-head of inspiration for us all."

Duryodhana agreed to the proposal of Karna. Then, he proceeded towards Drona who was surrounded by many Kings and warriors. He bowed low and said, "Revered Sir, I come to your refuge. You are peerless and matchless in skill, valour, wisdom and knowledge of war-fare. I beseech you to accept the command so that we are crowned with victory."

All the assembled Kings, Princes and warriors heartily endorsed the proposal put forward by Duryodhana. Drona gave his assent to their proposal. Duryodhana with great pride applied the ornamental mark of Commandership on the forehead of great Dronacharya amidst thunderous applause, renting the skies.

Drona remained in command for five days of the battle. Though he was old, yet he fought like a young soldier giving crushing defeat to Satyaki, Bheema, Arjuna, Abhimanyu, Drupada and Kashiraja, on a number of occasions.

Drona arrayed the army in a 'circular formation'. The Kaurvas had so much faith and confidence in his leadership that they thought as if they had already defeated the Pandavas. Karna who had been static under Bhishma's command, was now seen moving about in his great chariot on the battle-field with great courage and enthusiasm.

The Kaurva soldiers were inspired at the sight of Karna. They felt that the great Bhishma did not desire to kill the Pandavas, as he loved them from the core of his heart. But now, Karna would not spare them. Death was staring at them in the face.

In spite of his old age, Drona displayed great mettle on the battle-field like a young soldier. Whenever he launched a massive attack, the Pandava Forces scattered like clouds before a violent storm. He seemed to be invincible. He sent thousands of the Pandava soldiers to the abode of death, during his command, lasting for five days.

Ten days of fighting convinced Duryodhana that further fighting would spell his doom. So, he went to Drona and spoke thus, "We do not desire total victory. Could you oblige us by capturing the eldest Pandava alive and hand him over to us ?" Drona was filled with joy at such an intention of Duryodhana, as he himself hated the very idea of killing the Pandava brothers. So, the Acharya exclaimed, "Duryodhana, may God bless you ! How noble of you to refrain from killing Yudhishthira ! I will do my best to take him a prisoner and hand him over to you."

Drona thought that Duryodhana had undergone a change of heart. He wished to befriend the Pandavas. But the wicked Duryodhana had his own evil designs. It had become clear to him that the Pandavas could not be defeated on the battle-field.

So, fighting against them was futile. If the eldest Pandva was captured alive, he could be drawn into the battle of dice, once again and sent to the forests once more.

The news that Drona had assured Duryodhana to capture Yudhishthira alive that day, spread in the Pandava camp. So, all were alert to protect him from every side.

Drona launched a massive attack. He moved like lightning and destroyed the Pandava Forces like a fire, burning up dry logs. He showered arrows like the showers of rains. He converted the battle-field into a stage for the dance of the God of Death.

Then, his golden chariot sped forward straight to Yudhishthira who answered with barbed arrows.

But Drona could not be stopped. Yudhishthira's bow was cut down and Drona reached very close to him. Dhrishtadyumna tried to prevent his advance, but he was hurled aside. The whole army shouted that Yudhishthira was in the grip of Drona.

All of a sudden, the valiant Arjuna appeared on the battle-field. The ground rumbled under the wheels of his chariot which moved swiftly over bones and dead bodies, lying in heaps here, there and every where. The moment Drona saw Arjuna on the scene, he hesitated and held himself back.

A continuous stream of arrows, issued forth from the Gandiva. The battle-field was darkened by his flying shafts. Drona had to retreat. The battle was stopped for the day. Arjuna saved his eldest brother from the clutches of Drona. It was really a hair-breadth escape.

# 38. ABHIMANYU—THE MIGHTY MAN-AT-ARMS

Abhimanyu, the son of Arjuna and Subhadra was still, in his teens. But he was recognised as the equal of his father and uncle in the battle-field.

Yudhishthira sent for Abhimanyu and said to him, "Dear son, Drona today has arrayed his army in the 'lotus formation' since Arjuna is away. None except you can break Drona's formation. I ask you to do it or else we are doomed to be humiliated today in the absence of your father."

Abhimanyu replied, "I know how to penetrate this 'lotus formation' but I do not know how to come out of it, if the need arises."

Yudhishthira allayed his fears by saying, "Valiant lad, open a passage for us by breaking this impregnable array. The moment you break it, we too shall enter with you. So, the question of coming out of it does not arise at all. We shall smash the Kaurva warriors within the 'formation'." Abhimanyu at once ordered his charioteer Sumitra to drive fast towards Drona's division. The Pandavas followed Abhimanyu close behind him.

Abhimanyu rushed on like a young lion on a herd of elephants. The Kaurvas Forces scattered under his headlong onslaught. Drona kept on watching as Abhimanyu with the speed of lightning breached his 'formation' and entered into it. As Abhimanyu went in, the breach was closed by Jayadratha, the King of the Sindhu, who prevented the other Pandavas from entering the 'lotus formation'. As ill-luck would have it, Abhimanyu was isolated and he found himself all alone within that treacherous 'formation'. But he was undaunted. The lone warrior within caused widespread destruction of the Kaurva Forces. He covered the field with severed heads and limbs of the slain warriors.

The destruction caused by Abhimanyu enraged Duryodhana who pounced upon him like a tiger. If other warriors had not come to the rescue of Duryodhana, he would have fled to the abode of death. Abhimanyu now came down upon the rescuers and put them to headlong flight.

The desperate Kaurva warriors threw away all sense of shame and chivalry. A large number of their seasoned warriors launched a combined attack on the lone young hero. The brave lad was surrounded with enemies on all sides. Drona, his son Aswatthama, Kripa, Karna, Salya, Sakuni and so many others in their chariots dashed forward to kill the isolated young hero. But all of them were dashed back by Abhimanyu. They were baffled and broken. Karna's armour was pierced and Salya was badly wounded. Seeing Abhimanyu's valour in wielding his arms, Drona's eyes were filled with tears of affectionate admiration. Drona exclaimed to Kripa that there was never a fighter to equal Abhimanyu, the bravest boy.

A treachery was cooked to do away with Abhimanyu. Drona told Karna to attack him from behind. Karna obeyed. He shot an arrow from behind and broke Abhimanyu's bow. His horses and charioteer were killed. The disabled young warrior stood on the field with his sword and shield facing a number of enemies on all sides. Whirling his sword, he pushed them back in terror. They were confounded and dumb-founded. They felt as if his feet did not rest on the Earth. He seemed to be on wings in the air. At last, Drona shot an arrow that broke Abhimanyu's sword. His shield was torn to pieces, by Karna's sharp shafts.

Even then, Abhimanyu did not lose heart. He bent down and like lightning took up one of his chariot wheels. He whirled it like a discus to keep his enemies away. He was covered with dust falling from the chariot wheel. Vyasa says that the dust enhanced his natural beauty. While fighting fiercely, the young hero looked like a second Vishnu wielding his discus. But soon the chariot wheel too was shattered to pieces by the combined onslaught of so many great warriors. Then Dushasana's son sprang upon him. The two were engaged in a fatal duel. Both fell down together. But the son of Dushasana, managed to rise earlier than Abhimanyu. He picked up his mace and struck it hard on the armless hero who succumbed to the blow. All the noble men in the army were grieved at such a cruel and deceitful killing and tears rolled down their cheeks.

# 39. ABHIMANYU'S DEATH AVENGED, JAYADRATHA SLAIN

The brave Arjuna, the bereaved father, burst into heart-rending lamentation when he came to know that Abhimanyu, his dear son, had been killed in his absence. He was plunged into the ocean of grief.

Then, Krishna consoled his grief-stricken friend thus, "Beloved Partha, it does not behove you to grieve in this way. Our tribe has to live and die by weapons. Death is our perpetual companion. Fortunate are the warriors who die young on the battle front. Abhimanyu has brought great glory to himself as well as to all of us. He has attained celestial regions above. So, take heart and get ready to avenge Abhimanyu's death."

Thus, encouraged by Krishna, Arjuna took a solemn oath, "I will kill the wicked Jayadratha tomorrow before the Sun sets. If I fail to keep my pledge, I will burn myself alive." Then, he twanged his Gandiva string to which Krishana responded by blowing his *Panchajanya*.

As soon as the news of Arjuna's oath reached the enemy camp, Jayadratha was placed behind a strong army which Arjuna could not easily pierce. Drona placed Jayadratha and his force twelve miles to the rear of the main army. Bhurisravas, Karna, Aswatthama, Salya, Kripa and a host of other warriors were there to protect Jayadratha. Arjuna was so furious and forceful that none could prevent him from advancing forward at a terrific speed. Soon, he broke through all the Kaurva opponents and reached Jayadratha.

He was truly a 'great archer' who could discharge arrows from the Gandiva with his left as well as the right hand with equal ease and potency. So, he struck terror and confusion in the enemy camp.

The Kaurava warriors were non-plussed and felt as if death had visited the battle-field with her jaws wide-open to devour them. Only the poet-philosopher Vyasa can describe the combat that raged between Arjuna and the great warriors who were guarding the King of Sindhu, Jayadratha. None was able to stop Arjuna from reaching his prey.

The battle with Jayadratha raged long. It was not an easy task to defeat him. All of a sudden, there was darkness on the battle front and word went round that the Sun had set and Jayadratha was still alive. Shouts of joy were there in the Kaurva forces. At such a crucial moment, Krishna exclaimed to Arjuna, "Worry not, the Sun has not yet set. I have caused this darkness. Jayadratha is off guard and is looking at the western horizon. Now, it is the fittest moment to behead him."

70

An arrow flew swiftly from the Gandiva. It carried away Jayadratha's head abruptly like a vulture, swooping down on a chicken.

Then, Krishna asked Arjuna to send his shafts in rapid relays so that the head of Jayadratha might fall directly in the lap of his father, the sage, Vriddhakshatra.

Arjuna obeyed Krishna to the letter and spirit. He shot his wonderful arrows which were instrumental in carrying the head in the air. It was really an amazing feat to watch.

Vriddhakshatra sat with his eyes closed in his evening meditation.

The head of his son fell gently into his lap. As soon as, he got up after his meditation, the head fell to the ground with a thud. As ordained, the head of the old King burst into a hundred pieces. Both the son and the father together reached the abode of death.

Drona was bent upon annihilating the Pandava Army with his relentless attacks. Krishna invited the attention of Arjuna and said to him, "O Arjuna, Drona is invincible. But we must kill him either by hook or by crook. He can be desisted from fighting under only one condition. If he hears that his dear son Aswatthama is dead, all his interest in life will dry up and he shall throw down his arms. So, someone must tell Drona that his son has been killed."

Arjuna shuddered, as he could not tell a lie. No one wished to be a party to deceit. Yudhishthira resolved the dead-lock by telling Krishna that he was willing to bear this burden of sin. It was quite strange that a man of truth got ready to tell a lie for the first time in his life. But Lord Shiva swallowed the dreadful poison that was churned out of the ocean, simply to save the gods. Rama bore the sin of killing Vali from behind the trees to save his friend, Sugreeva. So, also Yudhishthira, the truthful, decided to commit this sin for the sake of others, when all the doors were barred.

Bheema picked up his huge iron mace. He brought it down with all his might on the head of an elephant, named Aswatthama who fell down dead. Then, Bheema approached Drona and roared loudly, "I have slain Aswatthama."

As soon as Drona heard the news of the death of his son, he stopped fighting and asked Dharmaputra if his son had really been killed.

Yudhishthira spoke aloud, "Yes, it is true that Aswatthama has been killed, "but it is the elephant." But the last words "it is the elephant" were not heard by Drona, as they were drowned in the din of drums.

That very moment the wheels of Yudhisthira's chariot which always moved four inches above the ground came down and touched the ground. Such was the impact of uttering a lie. The Dharmaputra too became a creature of the earth, for, he desired victory at any cost.

Knowing that his beloved son was no more, Drona lost the will to live. Throwing away his weapons, he sat down in Yoga meditation in his chariot and was soon in a trance or Samadhi.

At this juncture, Draupadi's brother, Dhrishtadyumna, drew out his sword. He climbed into Drona's chariot and chopped off the old warrior's head. A visible blaze of light mounted towards heaven.

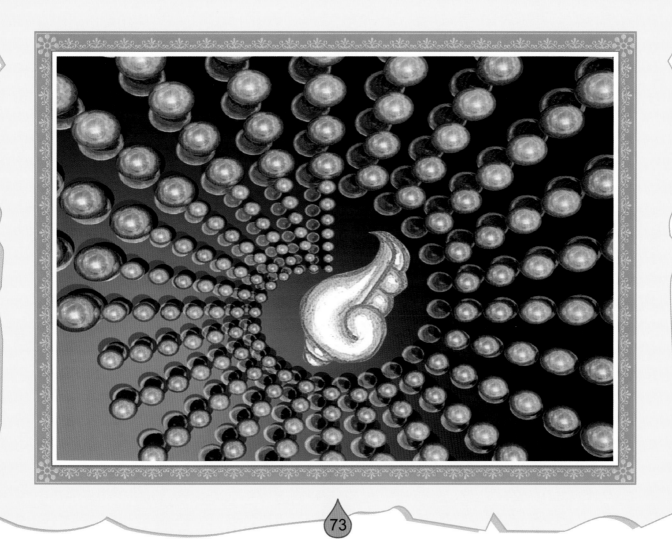

With Drona's exit from the battle-field of Mahabharata, Karna became the Chief Commander of the Kaurva Forces. Karna's chariot was being driven by Salya, the great.

Arjuna led the attack on Karna. Bheema followed Arjuna's chariot to give him support from behind. On the way, Dushasana attacked Bheema who did not lose the opportunity of killing him to redeem his pledge which he had taken thirteen years ago. Bheema was the very embodiment of Lord Yama, the Death God. He tore out Dushasana's arm with a mighty jerk and threw it bleeding on the battle-field. He then, sucked and drank the blood from his bosom like a beast of prey. Everybody on the battle-field shuddered with fear at such a horrible sight. Even the mighty Karna stood trembling. Salya advised Karna not to display any sign of fear. Like a gallant warrior, he should seek single combat with Arjuna.

Karna regained his suppressed spirits and mettle. With eyes red with rage, Karna ordered Salya to drive the chariot towards Arjuna. A terrible battle was fought between the two great archers. Karna, the son of Surya, shot a dazzling serpentine arrow, going straight to Arjuna at a terrific pace. Krishna was very vigilant and agile. He, at once, pressed the chariot down five fingers deep in the mud. The serpent-shaft just missed Arjuna's head but struck off his helmet. What a narrow escape thanks to Krishna !

Arjuna's wrath knew no bounds. He fixed a dart on his bow to do away with Karna. Verily, Karna's ill-fated hour had come. All of a sudden, the left wheel of his chariot sank deep into the bloody mire. He jumped down from his chariot to pull out the wheel from the fatal mud. He cried out to Arjuna to wait for a minute till he extricated the wheel. Karna now was reminded of the curse, pronounced on him by his preceptor Parusram that he would forget how to use his mighty weapons, just in the moment of his dire need. Karna again requested Arjuna to observe fair play and refrain from attacking him, as long as he was unarmed.

Krishna taunted Karna thus, "Look here, Karna ! you too swear by fair play and chivalry. Where was your chivalry when helpless Draupadi was being insulted by so many wicked warriors ? You cheated Dharamputra in gambling. Where was your fair play when isolated Abhimanyun was mobbed and killed by a number of Kaurva warriors including you ? Wicked man, it is unworthy of you to talk about fair play and chivalry.

Karna bent his head in shame without uttering a word. He quietly got into his chariot still stuck in mud and shot a mighty arrow which stunned Arjuna for a moment. Then, he jumped down again to lift the chariot wheel up. He pulled at it with all his might but the wheel did not budge even an inch.

Krishna cried out to Arjuna not to waste even a single moment in killing Karna. Arjuna obeyed and shot a sharp arrow which beheaded Karna. At first Arjuna's mind was wavering. He hesitated to attack an unarmed foe. But then, he accepted the command of the Lord who alone could bear the responsibility for breaches of Religion.

Here, we need to learn that the wrong should be put down through a sacred and unbiased war. The battle should be constantly fought for the sake of truth and justice.

# 42. THE COMBAT BETWEEN BHEEMA AND DURYODHANA

After Karna's death, Kripacharya spoke to Duryodhana thus, "Moved by greed and ambition, we threw our friends into the jaws of death. It is futile to follow this ruinous war. Let us make peace with the Pandavas."

But Duryodhana did not relish Kripacharya's advice.

The battle began under the supreme command of Salya who was as brave as a lion. Yudhishthira speared Salya to death. The surviving sons of Dhritarashtra joined hands together to attack Bheema who killed all of them.

Sahdeva shot a sharp sword-arrow which cut through Sakuni's neck like a sword. The head which was the root cause of all the wicked deeds on the part of the Kaurvas, rolled on the ground.

Now, the surviving soldiers of the Kaurvas fled the field to save themselves. Duryodhana who was left almost alone, took up his mace and moved towards a pool of water. He dived into it and held his breath under water. The Pandava brothers came running after him.

They called him a coward and a shameless fellow who was hiding in the pond to escape his death. Duryodhana replied from within the pond, "The Earth has nothing to attract me now. All my friends have been killed. My desire for kingdom has gone. You rule over the whole Earth without a rival."

Just see the irony of fate. Duryodhana who did not, allow even a needle point of land to the Pandavas was now willing to give them the kingship of the whole Earth. When many harsh, cruel and taunting words were hurled at Duryodhana, he came out of the pool with his mace in hand and said, "Since I am alone, come one by one to fight with me, single handed."

Now, the combat between Bheema and Duryodhana began. Their maces emitted sparks of fire when they clashed together. The battle continued for a long time as both were equal in strength and skill. Nobody knew who was going to win. Krishna asked Arjuna if Bheema had not vowed to break Duryodhana's thighs on which he had seated Draupadi. As soon as, Bheema overheard Krishna's words, he leapt like a lion with his mace in hand and hit hard on Duryodhana's thighs, shattering them to the ground. Then, Bheema danced a terrible dance on his body, lying low on the Earth.

Even while dying, Duryodhana did not repent for his misdeeds. He hurled abuses at Krishna who told him that his unbounded greed and lust for power were responsible for his destruction. Everybody must reap what he sows. He must not blame others for his downfall.

# 43. YUDHISHTHIRA COMFORTED

Dharmaputra's mind was in deep agony after winning the war. He lost all his kinsmen. Victory turned out to be a great defeat on account of losing so many talented human beings. He felt himself to be a great sinner. He felt like renouncing the world and going to the forest for undergoing penance to purify himself.

Narada and Vyasa comforted Yudhishthira and advised him to take up the burden of ruling the land with righteousness. He bowed to their wish.

So, Yudhishthira was duly crowned at Hastinapura. Before taking up the duties of the State, he went to the place where the learned Bhishma lay on his bed of arrows. He bowed low with reverence at his feet and sought his blessings, advice and instructions related to true religion.

It is the famous Shantiparva of the Mahabharta which records the conversation between King Yudhishthira and the great Bhishma.

# 44. PEARLS OF WISDOM, ENSHRINED IN THE GITA

It is needless to say that the Mahabharta which contains the Gita is called the fifth Veda, as it is a treasure house of all sorts of knowledge, concerning all the aspects and activities of mankind.

We have culled from this great epic peerless pearls of wisdom for the benefit and enlightenment of our readers. Bhishma advises Yudhishthira. Here are a few glimpses :

✦ "Always be up and doing. Never give way to lethargy and indolence. Destiny or fate alone cannot serve the purpose of a King. I assign topmost priority to human endeavour, as destiny is already preordained. Never get disheartened if obstacles and hurdles crop up in your way."

✦ "Truth is the greatest and the most precious ornament of a King. It ensures the confidence and faith of the people or the subjects in their King. The King should be the very embodiment of virtues, as the people follow in the footsteps of their King. A King should be humble as well as ruthless, according to the need of the hour. He must change his stand and behaviour, according to the exigency of the situation. Too much of a chatting with the servants is forbidden for a King."

✦ There are seven organs of a State—King, Minister, friends, treasure, land or country, fort and army. He who acts against the interests of any of these organs of the State deserves death whether he happens to be a teacher or a friend.

✦ "He who goes astray out of arrogance and follows the evil ways, must be punished by the King even though he happens to be his teacher."

✦ Had we heeded this glorious advice of Bhishma, our country would have been the leader of the world and our people would have lived in peace and prosperity.

✦ The eternal and perpetual duty of a King or the Government is to keep the people happy and satisfied. One should never give way to grief under any circumstances. All the riches of the world are fleeting. Nothing survives here. What you have is more important than what you have lost. Never grieve your losses. Grief cannot bring back your lost wealth.

✦ He who feels jealous of others, soon loses his health, wealth and peace of mind.

✦ Wealth is acquired by ceaseless industry and efforts. But even then, its nature is very fickle. So, the great thinkers go in for renunciation of wealth.

✦ All the pleasures and enjoyments of the world ultimately bring about the downfall of man. Few are the men born of noble parents who free themselves from the fleeting pleasures of the flesh. Some men are so stupid that they lose their life for their greed of wealth.

✦ When hoarding ends in depletion, life ends in death and meeting ends in parting; only a fool shall be enamoured of them.

✦ It is an inevitable fact that one day, either man gives up wealth or wealth takes leave of man. He who knows this fact, shall never be worried about wealth.

✦ Man alone can control his senses, his mind and tongue. He who does not control them wisely is doomed to destruction. Valour and wisdom ensure success in this world as well as in the next world. None is ever victorious and none is ever vanquished. Victory and defeat are transitory and momentary.

✦ One should not take them to heart. There is no teacher like a mother. The importance of a mother is ten times greater than that of a father.

✦ "The deed by which a son pleases his father; Brahmaji, the Creator is also pleased with that very deed."

✦ "The deed by which a son pleases his mother; the whole Earth is also worshipped by that very deed." It simply means that serving the mother means serving the whole Earth and serving the father means serving the Creator.

✦ "The deed by which a disciple pleases his teacher, God too is pleased and worshipped with it."

✦ "The teacher, the mother and the father are ever worthy of respect and reverence. They must never be insulted."

✦ "It is good to speak the truth. There is no virtue greater than truth. But if a lie saves the life of a good person, it should be considered as truth. If by speaking the truth, you endanger the life of a person, it should be treated as a lie."

✦ "It is none but one's true Religion which brings about prosperity and salvation."

✦ "A sinner is already dead by the force of his evil deeds."

✦ "A deceitful person should be tackled in a deceitful way."

✦ "Those who serve their parents are freed from all sorrows and sufferings."

✦ He who always speaks ill of others is a wolf in the guise of a man. He can never be at peace with himself. Avoid the company of such a person for good. He who is not frightened of others nor does he frighten others and he who desires nothing and does not feel jealous of anyone is fit for self-realization.

✦ "The best gift or charity is to confer fearlessness upon beings."

✦ "A learned man never gets angry. He does not bind himself with any attachment. He is not tossed by grief if something goes wrong or against him. He is not overjoyed to get his favourite things. He is not grieved when faced with a financial crisis. He remains as steadfast as the Himalayas by virtue of his very nature."

# Dreamland's Illustrated Religious Books

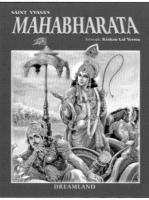
( Hard bound 200 pages, Price: Rs 350 )

( Hard bound 320 pages, Price: Rs 500 )

( Hard bound 80 pages, Price: Rs 200 )

( Hard bound 80 pages, Price: Rs 150 )

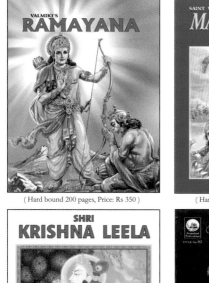
( Hard bound 96 pages, Price: Rs 200 )

( A set of 4 books, paper back, Price: Rs 25 each )

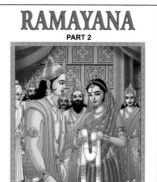
( A set of 12 books, paper back, Price: Rs 25 each )

( A set of 12 books, paper back, Price: Rs 25 each )

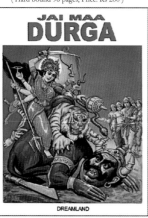
( Paper back, Price: Rs 50 )

( Paper back, Price: Rs 50 )

( Paper back, Price: Rs 50 )

( Paper back, Price: Rs 50 )

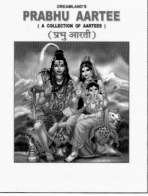
( Paper back, Price: Rs 50 )

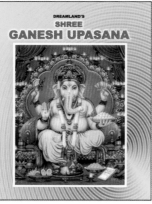
( Paper back, Price: Rs 50 )

( Paper back, Price: Rs 50 )

( Paper back, Price: Rs 50 )